THE VIEW FROM

INSIDE THE SUN

A Ray of Hope for the Future of Humanity

by

Gaynel Hamilton

ISBN: 9781079133257

For Humanity with Love

Acknowledgements

Thank you to my husband, Colin, for all the helpful suggestions (especially regarding what to leave out!); to my daughters, for their ruthless honesty regarding the finer points of grammar and cover design; to my editors, Barbara Doyle and Jane Middleton, for their tireless enthusiasm and encouragement; and to all the people who have told me to write this book: family, friends, students, learned professors and strangers encountered in health club changing rooms. Finally, I have got on with the job and here it is.

Contents

"The universe does not exist "out there," independent of us. We are inescapably involved in bringing about that which appears to be happening. We are not only observers. We are participators. In some strange sense, this is a participatory universe. Physics is no longer satisfied with insights only into particles, fields of force, into geometry, or even into time and space. Today we demand of physics some understanding of existence itself."

John Archibald Wheeler

"A human being is part of a whole, called by us 'Universe', a part limited in time and space. He experiences himself, his thoughts and feelings, as something separated from the rest - a kind of optical delusion of his consciousness."

Albert Einstein

"The Art of Peace is medicine for a sick world. There is evil and disorder in the world because people have forgotten that all things emanate from one source. Return to that source and leave behind all self-centred thoughts, petty desires and anger. Those who are possessed by nothing possess everything."

Morihei Ueshiba (founder of Aikido), in The Art of Peace

Introduction

Welcome Home

Imagine coming home. Really coming home. Imagine a place where you can take off your coat, kick off your shoes and settle into your own space: warm, secure, comfortable. Your real home. A place where you are loved unconditionally. A place where you can be completely yourself. A place where you can discover what 'being yourself' actually means.

Maybe that place is right here, right now – wherever you are. Maybe the whole 'home' thing has more to do with *what* you are than *where* you are. Maybe you are, already, home.

Who Is This Book For?

That's a very good question!

This book was written especially for you, of course, but who are you?

Who were you before you were given a name?

Who were you before you started thinking your very first thoughts about this world that you were born into?

Who were you before you collected the experiences and memories that helped to shape your character and gave you the view of yourself that you currently hold?

Who is it that has experienced this world through your senses all your life?

Who has noticed the changes as your body grew and developed, emotions came and went, opinions formed and shifted, ideas and images popped into your head and reason tried to sort them all out and make sense of it all? What, among all of that, remained unchanging?

Who is reading these words right now?

When you can answer these questions, the contents of this book will appear to be so obvious that you will feel you could have written it yourself.

It doesn't matter where you were born or where you live; what cultural setting has helped to shape your life so far; what religion, if any, you follow, or what beliefs you currently hold: this book is for you. The real you. The deep down you.

How Do I Know You?

How can I possibly claim to know the deep down you without meeting you face to face, without spending some time with you, without listening to what you have to say, without sharing some experiences with you, without thinking your thoughts or feeling your feelings?

That's a fair question and it would make perfect sense to ask it if your thoughts and your feelings were all that you are. It's true that I don't have the slightest clue about any of that. But suppose there's something more to you than any of that: something kind of awesome that goes way beyond the criteria we normally use to describe ourselves and each other.

I'm not talking about your individual personality, or all the mental and physical attributes that make you unique and special, though, of course, those things are very important. If we all looked identical, acted in exactly the same ways and had the same thoughts in our heads all the time, the world would be a boring and a seriously messed up place. We are not clones or pre-programmed robots obeying the orders of unseen programmers or some kind of collective hive mind.

We appear to have free will. We get to choose our own thoughts, and we can choose to celebrate our own personal qualities as we live together like perfect notes in a symphony, or like the different coloured threads in a tapestry: each one equally beautiful and special in its own way and each one essential, exactly the way it is.

That, in itself, is seriously awesome, and yet what I'm referring to is something more than this: something we all share; something we all have in common; something fundamental.

Something even deeper than the fact that we each have a body made of flesh and bones and blood; irrespective of our size, shape, gender, culture or the colour of our skin.

Something that unites us even more than the fact that we are all born, we all do our best to survive in this world, we all hurt sometimes and, eventually, we all die.

Something even more than the fact that we are all human, we all make mistakes sometimes and we are all capable of greatness.

Something above and beyond our shared need to avoid suffering, to be happy, to be free to live our lives in the way we choose and to keep our loved ones safe during the limited time we have on this planet.

True enough, these are all things we have in common - and they are all very compelling reasons for seeing ourselves as part of a global family and making an effort to get on with each other while we are here - but no, there is something even deeper than any of that: something which makes all of our perceived differences shrink in comparison.

That something, and how to discover it for yourself, is what this book is all about.

Knowing this one thing, we come to know each other and to know ourselves. More than uniting us as a species, this one thing allows us to realise that we were never actually separate in the first place.

Sages throughout history have told us that, one day, we will all come to this realisation and live together in peace. Some of them refer to this realisation as 'waking up'. Some of them call it 'enlightenment'. Whatever name we give it, this particular time in our history would probably be a good time for all of us to experience it, so that we can put aside our differences while we get down to some rather urgent business. This book is written for every man, woman and child living on the planet Earth at this time, in the hope that we can stop causing each other unnecessary aggravation and get on with the job of saving ourselves from extinction.

Sounds like a plan.

And yet we have a problem.

A Ship in the Sunlight

I remember reading a story once about an ocean liner, cruising along on a warm summer day. Everything seems fine at first but the ship is slowly sinking because it has a hole in the hull below the water line. The only person who has seen it is a small child who can't plug the leak alone and goes off to get help. Some of the passengers are dozing on deck while soaking up the sun and say it's the crew's job to deal with such matters. Some are hung-over from a party last night and are sleeping it off in their cabins. The crew are too busy with their own delegated jobs to spare any time to deal with leaks. The child tries to find the captain but discovers that he's not on board, and now there's a fire in the engine room and...there are no lifeboats on this ship! Assuming that the child can wake everyone up in time and get anyone to listen, it will now take a herculean effort from everyone on board working together if they are to save themselves from a watery or fiery demise.

Well OK, that's just a story, isn't it? A bit of a far-fetched story at that. Human beings would never act this way would they?

Well, perhaps not with ships, but when it comes to planets....

Why People Are Waking Up Now

A few years ago, this story would, pretty much, have described our situation here on spaceship Earth. Fortunately, we appear to have come on a bit since then. It may not seem like it but people are already waking up now. Individuals, and even some corporations, are recognising the physical challenges we face and directing their attention towards finding creative solutions.

Perhaps even more importantly, people are beginning to recognise that the root cause of our difficulties - our view of each other as separate and different from ourselves - is actually an extremely unhelpful and damaging, if very understandable, illusion. Those who have seen this tend to share a worldview that is all-inclusive: a view that focuses not on profit, power or superiority but on equality, compassion, cooperation and kindness.

We all have our different ideas about how to live our lives in this world and how to get along with the millions of different creatures who share the planet with us and have as much right to be here as we have. Don't worry, I'm not here to lecture you on biology or ecology. You already know all that stuff - you'd have to have been living out on one of the moons of Jupiter for the past half a century not to have noticed that we've not been doing the best job ever in the global caretaking department - so that's not what this book is about.

I don't need to remind you about our warming, pollution-clogged planet with its changing weather patterns, rising sea levels and dwindling resources. You may have read recent estimates suggesting that around a thousand species are becoming extinct each year and that we are now using the natural resources of 1.7 planets: our own share and that of our future grandchildren as well. You don't need me to tell you that we only have the one planet, we don't have any 'lifeboats' and there is no actual person running the ship.

You will have noticed not only that the politicians we put in charge of different bits of it seem unable to agree with each other on how to save the world, but also that some of them seem to be hell-bent on putting every obstacle they can in the way of those who are trying to do so. You already know about the wars and the genocides and the unequal distribution of wealth and you may well be asking why it is that we seem to put more effort into developing, selling and using weapons than into understanding each other and working together in what could otherwise be the last few years of our residence on the planet Earth.

But I'm not here to spread more doom and gloom. You get enough of that already every time you watch the news. What I am here to offer is hope.

This book doesn't set out to make anyone wrong; it's about seeing a bigger picture that allows us to look at the world with fresh eyes, to see how things actually are, and then think about what we can do together to make things right.

My hope is that you will continue to read these words to the end of this book and that, by doing so, you will glimpse something you may not have seen before: something that will perhaps make some sense of this crazy situation we have gotten ourselves into.

But first, another ship story, which I think I first heard from the famous Stephen Covey, author of *The 7 Habits of Highly Effective People.*

A Ship in the Dark

On a dark, foggy night, the captain of a battleship is standing on deck when he notices a flashing light in the distance. After a few minutes, he realises that the other ship is on a collision course with his own. So he calls his signalman and orders him to send a message to the other ship, warning it to change course by twenty degrees.

The signal is sent. A few moments later the signalman reports that the flashing light in the distance is telling the captain that it will not change course but suggests that his own ship should change course by twenty degrees.

The light is closer now and the captain is becoming alarmed and more than a little bit annoyed. He sends the signal: "I am a captain. Change course twenty degrees!"

The reply: "I am a Lieutenant. Change course by twenty degrees!"

The captain by now is furious. "I am a battleship! Change course twenty degrees!"

Back comes the signal: "I am a lighthouse".

That's called a paradigm shift.

This book is intended to allow you to experience a paradigm shift for yourself. Call it 'enlightenment' if you want to, or maybe call it a new, interesting and possibly helpful way of looking at things.

Whether it brings about an "Aha!" moment, a "Well duh!" moment or a "WTF?" moment will depend largely on where you are right now and how much of what follows you have already seen for yourself. My hope, however, is that we can all, eventually, get to a place where we can agree on one thing and, whichever path we took up the mountain, when we are all standing at the top, the view we share will be well worth the climb.

The Illusion of Separation

"The attempt to live according to the notion that the fragments are really separate is, in essence, what has led to the growing series of extremely urgent crises that is confronting us today."

David Bohm

One of the most widely-held beliefs in the world today is that we are all separate. This idea of separation gives rise to all kinds of problems, from jealousy and crime to war and genocide. Such things are only possible if we see ourselves as discrete entities, different from each other. Even those of us who have faith in some kind of over-arching power or entity, which many of us call "God", usually see this supreme being as separate from ourselves.

Where did the idea of separation come from? It's an easy enough conclusion to draw, since each of us appears to be a temporary bundle of blood, bone, muscle and other stuff, surrounded by skin. However, now that we have known, for at least the last hundred years, that the universe is an energy field and that we are all made from the same stuff, are we still justified in thinking of ourselves as separate from everything, including our God if we happen to have one? Is that not a recipe for loneliness, suffering and conflict?

So what's the alternative? What insights have we, as a species, come up with so far that might answer our questions about what we are and what 'reality' might be? And even if this can be explained in a way that we can all understand, how do we come to grasp the relevance of it in our own lives?

I'm going to start by attempting to describe to you something that happened to me back in 1993: a sudden change in perspective that changed my life. It is my hope that, by sharing this with you and by going on to discuss some of the things I have learned as a result of that experience, I might offer you an insight that will not only help you to feel happier and perhaps find more meaning in your life, but may also help us all to evolve as a species at this critical stage in our history and so enable us to leave a world fit to live in for those who come after us.

> *"A man said to him, "Tell my brothers to divide my father's possessions with me." He said to him, "O man, who has made me a divider?" He turned to his disciples and said to them, "I am not a divider, am I?""*
>
> *The Gospel of Thomas, Verse 72*

How I Woke Up

The event I'd like to tell you about took place in September 1993 but, just to set it in a proper context, I need to start with a little bit of background about my life up to that point.

Like many people, from as far back as I can remember, I had a burning need to know what I was and where I came from. In fact, laying in my pram before I even learned to talk, I'm sure that, for a moment there, I knew. I remember thinking how obvious it was and that I wouldn't forget this time, and then watching it slip away and feeling very frustrated that I had already forgotten what I had just decided not to forget! I knew it was very important but it just slid away in the way that dreams do when you wake up. Anyway, I was left with a thirst for knowledge that continued throughout my childhood and teens. I wanted to know, for example, why a blade of grass feels the way it does, how it grows, why it's here, and where is here anyway?

I was sent to church and Sunday school and the attached Church of England primary school, where I duly accepted the offered facts and fictions in equal measure (I was eleven before I got the inside gen on Santa) while becoming increasingly frustrated by the seeming inability of grown-ups to answer the most important questions, like "Where did the universe come from?" and "What is flame?" I spent ages looking into our coal fire and trying to fathom out that one!

Science lessons may or may not have helped but I was not allowed to do physics or chemistry at O Level because, apparently, those were 'boys' subjects'. Suffering, as I was, from the double misfortune of being a girl and lacking the saving grace of being considered to be particularly gifted at mathematics, I was allowed to study biology which was not, at that time, considered to be a 'proper science'. So I gate-crashed the lunchtime physics club and duly got kicked out by the deputy head for causing disruption by asking awkward questions like: "What is flame?"

Though the physics teacher came across as, potentially, more informed about such matters than anyone else I knew at the time, the answers he gave were far from satisfying. Fire, apparently, was energy. So what was energy? The capacity to do work. And so it went on, each answer leading to another statement containing terms requiring further definition and thereby raising more questions, until in the end, having circled back to the thorny problem of energy and where it might have come from in the first place, he blurted out: "Only God knows that!", at which point, I was duly removed by the deputy head and warned never to return, on threat of detention and a range of alternative consequences that did not outweigh my embarrassment at being labelled the worst behaved girl in the school again.

So the hunt for answers continued. I attended confirmation classes at the church, prior to being paraded in front of the bishop in a white dress, and was gutted to find that, whether God knew the answers to my questions or not, the vicar certainly didn't! So I gave up religion. The best that came out of my supposed 'spiritual' education was being allowed to collect the key to the church from the vicarage and let myself in. I just sat there on a front pew and had a go at talking to God myself and waited for some kind of evidence that He was listening.

I didn't hear any voices, you may or may not be relieved to know. It was kind of disappointing at the time but somewhat reassuring now.

It was very peaceful though. I had been doing yoga since the age of four, courtesy of our PE teacher, and had attempted to teach myself to meditate at around the age of ten, as per instructions gleaned from a small yoga book acquired from a supermarket checkout. This helpful guide also advised me to never take mind-altering substances, so that if I did have a mystical experience, I would know it to be authentic. I still don't drink coffee. The instructions said that I should lay on my back in the 'corpse position' for twenty minutes without thinking. Easy, eh?

After months of laying on my back on the rug at the bottom of my bed, I thought, "This is it! I'm not thinking about anything now!" Then I realised that I was still thinking about not thinking. Keeping the mind quiet, I discovered, was not as easy as it sounded but, sitting quietly in the church, waiting patiently for the voice of God, I was probably closer to the meditative state than during any of my previous efforts.

At seventeen, I was learning more Yoga and some Tai Chi from a fortnightly magazine, called *Come Alive*, that I collected in binders.

At school I was missing lessons and escaping to the library, where I continued my search for answers in the words of poets and philosophers and anyone else who might be expected to know about such things.

As to career choices, I wanted to do everything I could to save the world from its seeming downward spiral of overpopulation and resulting environmental catastrophe. Books, such as Paul Ehrlich's *The Population Bomb* and Gordon Rattray Taylor's *The Doomsday Book* and *The Biological Time Bomb*, left me in no doubt about the global predicament we were facing, but talking to people about rainforest destruction, exponential population growth and rising sea levels, in the area I grew up in at least, was likely to earn you the dubious title of 'tree-hugger' or just plain potty.

I was sure that there were like-minded people further afield - as evidenced by the existence of organisations such as Greenpeace, Friends of the Earth and the World Wildlife Fund, which I duly joined - but those were the days when communication, with anyone more than a short bus-ride away, was limited to writing letters, or finding a phone box that was still working and then speaking for as long as you could manage before you ran out of loose change. Computers were boxes the size of dining halls that were fed information via little cards with holes in them, and the internet was yet to be thought of.

Nevertheless, my horizons were widening and my plan, from the age of about thirteen, was to become a game warden in Africa so that I could make a start on my efforts to improve the world by protecting wildlife. My careers adviser duly advised me to let go of such silly ideas and do something sensible such as become an actress, on the grounds that my greatest claim to fame, thus far, was that I could sing! So, of course, on leaving school, I went off to be a game warden in a safari park and ignored subsequent requests from the careers mistress to write an article for the school magazine on "my exciting new life".

After a while, I got married, went to College (where I finally got to study maths, physics and chemistry), worked in various laboratories in an attempt to do something about environmental pollution (Water Authority) and animal conservation (Ministry of Agriculture) and did various Open University courses in science subjects. I eventually signed up for a few years of evening classes in philosophy and went to university full-time to get an honours degree in biochemistry and various post graduate qualifications in education and psychology, while I had children and became a full-time lecturer.

And while all that was going on, I was studying the words of the wise, from *The Tao Te Ching* to *The Bhagavad Gita*. I kept delving deeper and deeper, studying the works of Paul Brunton (his *The Hidden Teaching Beyond Yoga* kind of jumped off the shelf at me at the library and I actually collected all of his posthumously-assembled notebooks) and everything else I could lay my hands on, from the poems of Rumi to *The Upanishads* and the teachings of the Buddha.

A lot of what I read sounded deeply mysterious and complex, and probably important, but the actual meaning of it remained just out of reach. Most of the supposedly enlightening, yet tortuous, paths on offer to the humble seeker seemed guaranteed to keep one bogged down in a quagmire of exotic terminology and esoteric practices for at least several lifetimes. Underneath it all, however, there was a common theme of the unity of everything, the existence of a supreme Self and the importance of loving the said overarching divine being. But what was the relevance of this to everyday life? If God was a thing, why so much suffering? If there was only the One Self, what was I? (I know, "well duh!" right?)

I meditated dutifully for twenty minutes, twice a day (when I remembered) but, apart from feeling very peaceful, what was supposed to happen if I ever got to the state of 'nirvana'? Mystery upon mystery.

At that time, I had only vague ideas about the relevance of quantum physics to any of my spiritual questings. At university, we had looked at quantum mechanics in the second year and learned how to stuff numbers into the Schrödinger equation and get answers out that would allow us to pass exams, but the significance of what it all meant had gone sailing right on over my head. I was yet to open my eyes to the fact that reality is not at all what we think it is.

By the early nineties, I had learned a lot of stuff and seen a pattern emerging within it. I had meditated with proper meditators, had a real Chinese master teaching me Tai Chi and had discussed truth and reality with actual philosophers, and yet I was still bursting with questions, though now feeling as if the answers were tantalisingly close, like I was teetering on the edge of something and just that little bit more information would make sense of it all. I had also discovered that too much meditation could be pathological because it made you feel cut off from the world, like a ghost, if you did it all the time, so now I only did it occasionally.

On one such occasion, in the mid-eighties, while sitting at my desk in my bedroom, I stopped working and sat still for a few moments to meditate. Instead of simply clearing my mind and just resting in the stillness as usual, I let my attention go right out and imagined expanding beyond the house, the city, the country, until I could see glaciers collapsing into the sea on the coast of Greenland and see the sun beyond the curve of the horizon and the Earth rolling beneath me. I went back and back until I could see the planets, the stars, the galaxies and, eventually, the whole universe, which shrank to a tiny speck in front of me and only existed because I was resting my attention on it, otherwise it would just disappear and there would be nothing. Nothing except myself. And what was that? Just pure awareness without a body and nothing to be actually aware of. Then what?

It occurred to me that this was how God must be and (this will sound ridiculous but it's how it was) I felt so sorry for Him! How must it be to be so completely alone? I had a belief (probably gained from a study of Bhakti Yoga) that if I loved God enough, I would unite with Him but, I realised, that would mean becoming Him. Did I love God so much that I could share His loneliness?

The thought of that much aloneness was worse than the fear of pain or dying. I suppose it was a bit like loving a prisoner in solitary confinement but not yet being ready to step into the cell and take their place (though there was, of course, no cell and, though it was not obvious to me at that time, no two separate entities).

So I plunged myself back into the universe and deferred thinking about it for the time being. Though this little flight of the imagination was not life-transforming, just a bit disturbing, it probably set the scene for what was to follow.

I'm sure I'm not the first person to have engaged in this type of fantasy. I expect that many others have done it too. There are videos on YouTube showing rather beautiful simulations of the same sort of thing. I'm not sure how many people emerged from it feeling sad for God though. Clearly, this was not enlightenment, whatever that was! The search continued.

Then, in September of 1993, several things happened. Firstly, I managed to fall down our back steps. Thanks to a wrecked knee and ankle and an over-enthusiastic bit of bandaging, I ended up in hospital with a deep vein thrombosis – a blood clot in my leg – and found myself unattended on a trolley in a dimly-lit corridor for several hours in the middle of the night. I had been provided with the information that a bit of the blood clot in my leg could break off at any time and travel to my heart to give me a heart attack, or to my brain to give me a stroke, or to my lungs to give me a pulmonary embolism, any one of which could kill me. I was told that if I felt a pain going across my abdomen, that meant it was going to my lungs and that would probably be the end of me.

I did not have a buzzer, I had not been offered any type of anticoagulant medication and there was nobody around in the corridor, so I just lay there waiting for the pain that would tell me I was about to die. I didn't know if I had hours, minutes or seconds left in this world. I was heartbroken because I had just said goodbye to my two young children, perhaps for the last time, before leaving home, and worried because I had not made a will. On top of that, I was very concerned about my forthcoming encounter with the Grim Reaper. I wanted to talk to someone wise about what happens when you actually die, but there was no one there to talk to, wise or otherwise. I had told the person filling in the admission forms that I had no religion and they had said: "C of E then," and written that down, so it was unlikely that they would find me an enlightened being if I asked for one. The best I could do was to weep for my children and attempt to make peace with my maker.

Seconds passed. Minutes passed. Hours crept by. Still alive so far...

Sometime in the depths of the night, I was taken upstairs to a ward, where the nurses catalogued the few belongings I had with me in a special book, something that had never happened before and which I took to mean that they were not expecting me to make it through to morning. An hour or so later, a lady in the bed diagonally opposite mine passed away and was taken out on a trolley while I lay there, shocked and saddened by her sudden demise and expecting to be following her soon.

Of course, the blood clot remained happily where it was and I lived to tell the tale, but it was a very different me that watched the sun come up the next morning. From that moment onwards, I never took life for granted again. I felt so incredibly lucky to be seeing that sunrise. Things that were once unpleasant, like putting the car in the garage in the winter winds and rain, were now a joy to me because they reminded me that I was alive. I was thankful for each new experience, especially seeing the crocuses and blossoms emerge in the spring, which I had thought I would never see again. Every moment with my children was precious. Indeed, I had another baby who would never have been born if things had gone differently that night.

It could be said that I was never in that much danger in the first place and my perception of the imminence of death was exaggerated as a result of the way the hospital staff handled my admission but, in some ways, I am grateful for that, because having what I perceived to be such a close call made me so much more appreciative of whatever time I had left and determined to use it wisely to help other people in whatever ways I could as a kind of "thank you" for being given a second chance. I also felt a kind of calm acceptance. If it was possible to merge with the universal consciousness when I died, then so be it.

The next day, in hospital, I read Shantanand Saraswati's book, *Good Company*, with its metaphorical stories of the meditative state, and imagined my body as a jar that, when empty, could be immersed in a river of light. Maybe the jar itself would ultimately dissolve into the light. I went home and set about reading two books: *The Tao of Physics* and *The Dancing Wu Li Masters*.

I was about half way down a page towards the end of the latter, in the middle of a paragraph about David Bohm's ideas on wholeness and the 'implicate order', and reflecting on the implications of string theory, when I experienced a sudden paradigm shift. It was not that everything changed around me, it was just that the way I was looking at everything changed. It was like putting on a new pair of glasses, or maybe like taking off a pair of shades I never needed in the first place and seeing things properly for the first time.

I will do my best to describe this but I'm not sure that words are adequate.

In my mind's eye, I had an image of a kind of ocean of light, neither bright nor dim, more like a gentle dawn going on and on, in all directions, forever. Within this, the light could gather into patterns, giving rise to stars and planets and people. In texture, it seemed a bit like the shimmering you get on a television that's not tuned in to any channel, but so much finer, and everything was connected to everything else because things were all continuously arising as patterns within the light and returning to it and were never, at any time, separate from it. It was all just one, this symphony playing at the surface of silence, this sea of vibration emerging from stillness, this nothing that was somehow also everything. It was, as Saraswati had said, "like light vibrations that are everywhere present".

And I realised that I am that - and so are you, and so is everything. It's not like what philosophers call solipsism. You are not a figment of my deranged imagination. You are yourself and I am myself and yet, ultimately, we are both that same self that is both everything and nothing.

It was not a case of "that is over there and I am over here and I need to somehow merge with it", it was "this is what I am, what I have always been and what I always will be". There was never any separation in the first place. There was bliss. There was love: not like

18

the attachment or attraction of one person to another but simply as the nature of the whole.

It was not spectacular. There were no blaring trumpets or choirs of angels, yet it was what young people today would call an OMG moment in which my perception of pretty much everything shifted and all the knowledge I had gathered from a lifetime of searching just fell into place like pieces in a jigsaw puzzle. I could see now what lay at the core of many religions yet had been overshadowed by misinterpretation and dogma; what science was attempting to understand and measure; what sages, mystics and saints had written about for millennia; yet if I had told the average priest what I was seeing, I would probably have inspired blank stares or concerns about my sanity.

At the time, I burst out laughing. It was all just so blindingly obvious that I couldn't believe how dense I'd been in not seeing it before. Days later, I was still grinning widely and prone to occasional chuckling. Maybe it's because it is so obvious, so ordinary and so very familiar that it is so easy to overlook when one is striving to become 'enlightened'. As Daikaku said: "When you come to grasp it, you find that it was ever before your eyes… You know then that your heart is so vast that it can never be measured." There is no glory or status to be gained by seeing it. If anything, there is increased humility. Being only one, there is no one to impress but oneself.

From then on, it was a case of "what use is a well when water flows everywhere?" as it says in the *Bhagavad Gita*. The wise men and women throughout the world and throughout history were all describing the same thing and there was an overlap between the words of scientists and sages. Guru Nanak's "As a million sparks rise from a single fire and fall back into it," and Lao Tze's "continually emerging, it returns again and again to nothingness" pretty much summed up the "continual dance of creation and annihilation" described by quantum physicists. There was Erwin Schrödinger saying: "The overall number of minds is just one" and Max Planck saying: "This mind is the matrix of all matter". I actually had shivers up my spine the first time I read *The Gospel of Thomas*: "Split a piece of wood and I am there. Lift up a stone and you will find me there". Of course! Two thousand years melted away in an instant and the one mind continued to know itself.

Although the insight only lasted in its fullness and clarity for the rest of that afternoon, during which time I had a go at describing it by writing a poem, I could bring it to mind at any time, just by switching attention from the individual viewpoint to the universal. As Sogyal Rinpoche said: "Once you have the view, you will be like the sky; empty, spacious and pure from the beginning".

Here is the poem I wrote that afternoon:

Full, its contents have no substance.

Empty, it contains all things.

Silent, its music is unending.

Still, it dances the eternal dance.

Without heat, it is not cold.

Without light, it is not dark.

Look for it, there is nothing to be found.

Look away from it, it cannot be escaped.

Vast, its smallness is beyond conception.

20

Tiny it holds infinity within.

Unity, it holds numbers beyond reckoning.
Limitless, its wholeness is complete.

Ancient, it is forever new
Eternal, all of it is now.

Vibrations arising, evolving, dissolving,
Interrelations of form without form,
Shifting, holding, changing, returning,
Transient threads in the fabric of all.

There is nothing to grasp...
There is everything to be

With this view in mind, there was no possibility of racism or other types of prejudice, since every person was simply a different aspect of the same Self. At the time, I called this "absolute equality", though some people thought this was nonsense. What I meant was that hating anyone would be like your left hand hating your right hand or your thumb feeling an aversion to your little finger just because it looked a bit different. We are all one. Ethical behaviour and compassion for all living creatures arises naturally from this awareness, rather than being required as part of any religion. If you harm anyone or anything, you are harming yourself. If we could all see this, there would be no reason for fighting; no possibility of exploiting the planet's resources for personal gain. The world, I realised, needs to wake up now.

I was hopeful that quantum physicists would take the lead in opening people's eyes in ways that religious leaders had not yet managed to do. Sadly, many scientists seemed unaware of the implications of their findings, though I am hopeful that they will, one day, make the leap that unifies their various viewpoints and allows a majority of people to share a knowledge of the truth, not simply as information but through direct experience.

What we need is not a "my religion is better than your religion" approach (personally, I don't have one but I'm not an atheist either, which people tend to find confusing), nor an ongoing dispute between science versus religion. What we need is an overarching view that includes all of it, recognises the inherent truth underlying it and makes sense of it all without making anyone wrong or leaving them feeling silly, undervalued or outcast.

What difference has all of this made in my life? Well to begin with, it changed how I feel. Up to that point I had been frantically searching for an elusive something or someone, be it knowledge, 'enlightenment', 'Mr Right' or even God. I had felt a kind of yawning, aching emptiness inside. After that day, there was an inner contentment. Life was not without its considerable challenges, not least of which are the heartaches that arise from the sufferings of one's children and elderly relatives and the constant struggle to help them to be safe and happy on a daily basis. All of this continues of course, since life is like that, whatever you perceive about the nature of ultimate reality. Even when you know it's a game you still have to learn the rules and get on with playing it: you can't just take your bat and ball and go home. As it says in the *Bhagavad Gita*, on the field of truth, on the battlefield of life: "you cannot say "I will not fight": nature will compel you to!" But inside, I was basically happy and I was no longer afraid of dying.

Since then I have continued to do whatever work I can to help people, mainly through teaching. While being very careful not to found some kind of cult or set myself up as some kind of guru, I have continued to study widely, especially in the fields of physics and psychology and, with my husband, I have helped thousands of people to improve their health and quality of life well into their retirement and perhaps to find some degree of peace and meaning on the way.

Now, however, I am being asked by many people to write a book – this book – to share everything I have discovered during my long search for "the truth", in the hope that it will bring happiness to many.

"Society will not change by compulsion. It requires a change of heart. Understand that nothing is your own, that all belongs to all. Then only society will change... Every cause is universal. Your very body will not exist without the entire universe contributing to its creation and survival."

Nisargadatta

Before We Start

"The four difficulties of realising Enlightenment:
So close you can't see it.
So deep you can't fathom it.
So simple you can't believe it.
So good you can't accept it."
Tibetan Proverb

It could be said that 'enlightenment' is the process by which knowledge as information meets knowledge as direct experience, just as a match rubs against the sandpaper of a matchbox. The resulting flame is the paradigm shift that illuminates what was once hidden in darkness.

You may be on your own quest right now, looking for the catalyst that will bring about that illumination. Somewhere among the following pages, you may come across the words that bring everything together. It could happen suddenly, or it could just evolve slowly and steadily as you are reading, or some time afterwards, perhaps when you are meditating or when you notice that other people are speaking about the same thing.

We can increase the probability of this happening by having access to the right kind of information in the first place. We can glean this from many sources, including the insights of scientists, philosophers and sages. We may even find the spark that ignites that flame in a religious text or a piece of artwork.

The boundaries between science, religion and art are not as clear-cut as we might think. All three attempt to understand, describe and express reality; they just go about it in different ways. While a scientist attempts to measure it and to express it mathematically, a religious person might feel it intuitively and attempt to express it in prayer or song and an artist may experience it as a presence working through them, expressing itself in the creation of a great masterpiece of literature, music or visual art - and of course these may overlap. Many great artists, like Leonardo Da Vinci, have also been scientists and many scientists have, like Einstein, set out to "know the mind of God". Philosophers embrace the whole lot and look for the truth in everything.

I have appreciated many long and fruitful discussions with scientists, artists, religious leaders, philosophers and devout atheists. It is only by engaging in honest debate about seemingly diverse matters that we demolish, layer by layer, the edifice of our inherent prejudices and superficial differences. Ultimately, we may come to glimpse the one thing that all of us have in common: the one thing that lies at the heart of each and every one of us, the seeing of which shakes our core beliefs to their foundations and renders all further debate superfluous.

That is what this book is about.

So, as we set out on our quest to find the truth underlying reality, we can prepare the way by looking at what scientists, philosophers and sages are able to tell us so far that could be useful for us to know during our journey, but first we need to be very clear about what we mean when we use words like 'enlightenment', 'truth', 'philosophy', 'science', 'reality' and 'spiritual paths'.

What is Enlightenment?

'Enlightenment' is one of those awkward words that mean different things to different people. It's the kind of word that can make people sound as if they know what they are talking about, even when they are talking nonsense.

There is a name for words like these: they're called 'nominalizations'. Politicians use them all the time. They have no intrinsic meaning in themselves but they can make a speech sound very impressive so you feel that you really should be able to follow what is being said and a little bit dim if you don't. If you listen to a TV interviewee spouting on for twenty minutes, sounding very learned yet completely avoiding answering any of the questions asked, it will probably be as a result of the nominalizations they threw in there to side-track your attention. You may even attach your own meaning to words like 'issues' and 'challenges' so that they match your existing hopes and expectations and make you feel like this guy is on your side rather than waffling on about nothing in particular. It's how the experts hypnotise crowds and end up running countries.

Nominalisations, then, are responsible for much of the BS that we encounter in this world. The only way to deal with words like this is to unwrap them. So if someone says: "A vote for me is a vote for change"; instead of just assuming that they are promising to make the specific changes that we personally want to see, which may be highly unlikely, we might reasonably ask: "Change what?" "Change it to what?" and "How do you intend to go about that?"

So in this book, in order to achieve the task I have set myself of keeping it BS-free, I will attempt to avoid the trap of generating endless strings of empty words, as is so often the case in 'spiritual' books, speeches and sermons.

Some spiritual teachers and their followers may get caught up in language that is designed to clarify their perception yet just fogs up the conversation. In an attempt to prove that their awakening experience was 'authentic', they will say things like "awareness says this" or "awakening says that" or "presence says the other", so that people listening know that it is not their own, supposedly dissolved, ego that is talking at that moment but the higher, universal being. Some may become very cynical about the claims of others to have awoken and judge a temporary awakening to be inferior to a permanent awakening. While some 'mystical' experiences can be more lasting or enjoyable, however, becoming enlightened is not a scale of illumination. It's more of an either/or thing. Just as you can't be slightly dead or slightly pregnant and a needle can't be slightly sterile, you can't be slightly enlightened. Like the story of the lighthouse, you either know or you don't know and once you know, you can't un-know, even if you choose to go back to sleep for a while and run your battleship onto the rocks.

So, let's start by unwrapping the word 'enlightenment'. On its own, it makes little sense. If we are hoping to become enlightened, it's necessary to specify what it is that we are seeking to be enlightened about. I could be seeking to gain some clarification about how to make pizza or how to fill in my tax form and consider myself to be duly enlightened when I receive the appropriate information.

I could say that we will be discussing 'spiritual enlightenment' but even the word 'spiritual' is a nominalization that a thousand people will interpret in a thousand different ways, from communing with ghosts to deeply mystical experiences - assuming that we can all agree on what we mean by 'ghost' and 'mystical' - and on it goes.

When I refer to enlightenment here, I will be talking about gaining a direct and lasting insight into what is real…and here we go down the next rabbit hole, because even the word 'reality' can be thought of as a nominalisation!

As we will see from the following pages, we may all be under the impression that we have a pretty good idea about what is real but if you were to ask a bunch of the world's top scientists and philosophers what 'reality' is, the only thing they might agree on is that none of them really know, though they will be more than willing to tell you what it isn't and give you lots of suggestions as to what it might be. 'Reality' is incredibly difficult to pin down, despite everyone's best efforts to date. From string theory and loop quantum gravity to cosmic holographic computer simulations and the idea that everything is an illusion, there are innumerable possibilities and few hard and fast conclusions.

Even if we ever get to the point where we fully understand all the physical laws of the universe and someone comes up with the long-sought Theory of Everything, we will still find that each of us has a different take on what is real at any given moment.

So, as you can see, our explorations of the nature of reality will be challenging enough without adding any deliberately esoteric BS to fog the debate. In fact, there may be some who think it would be better not to venture into this subject at all, due to a widespread view that spiritual enlightenment cannot and should not be talked about. Various reasons are given for this but the most common one is the assertion that there are no words to describe this state, so those who claim to know don't really know. Which then also leaves open the possibility that the person who claims not to know indeed doesn't!

We hear stories of various gurus who have withdrawn from the world and maintained silence rather than attempt to speak about the indescribable. If they don't speak about it, how can anyone know that they were 'enlightened' in the first place? In any case, what use is enlightenment if all we do with it is sit in a cave, or billion dollar estate, all day? If there are indeed illumined beings, wiser than the rest of us, might it not be useful to have them walking among us and offering advice on what to do about our present predicament, rather than retiring to distant retreats and leaving us to it?

Statements such as: "He who claims to know, knows nothing; he who knows nothing, knows" can be interpreted in different ways. Maybe it doesn't mean that the wise go around pretending not to know anything and the answers are best sought from those with the lowest IQ; perhaps it means that when we truly know what 'nothing' is, we will realise that, as Kalu Rinpoche said: "We are no thing, and being no thing, we are everything."

Perhaps it's time for more of those who 'know' to speak out and help the human race to wake up. Admittedly, some of them have been shouting it from the rooftops for millennia and few of us have ever listened. Many of those who have listened have misinterpreted their words in ways that would elicit face palms or tears from the illumined ones, assuming that they survived long enough to raise palms to their faces and had not been immediately dispatched to the afterlife as a reward for their outpourings. Maybe that's why some of them have felt a need to hide away in caves.

Maybe, in this age of the internet and greater tolerance, we can learn to be better listeners, though if a messiah were to appear among us, we would probably deny him or her access to most countries for having the wrong colour of skin, or locked away in a psychiatric hospital for being delusional, or incarcerated in some dark prison for being a dissident, or simply mocked, ignored or stoned for being the wrong gender. Our ability to stereotype even heavenly messengers knows no bounds.

Enlightenment, in my own opinion, can mean casting a light on what was previously obscured by darkness. It can also be described as becoming lighter, as if by shedding a load. I remember feeling an overwhelming sense of relief at shedding the burden of all that seeking! When something becomes obvious to you, it just is. "What type of boat is it? Why doesn't it change course? Why is that guy so stubborn? Oh. It's a lighthouse. Fair enough."

The process of waking up does not need to be confined to those few rare individuals who have spent lifetimes devoted to their spiritual quest. Potentially, we can all wake up right now. We can all gain a little more light with which to view things more clearly. We can all, perhaps, feel a little lighter by shedding some of the heavy load we have been carrying on our shoulders, especially the burdens of fear and hatred that harm ourselves even more than the people we hate and fear. We can come to understand the truth intellectually and we can come to experience it for ourselves.

We will need a fair amount of patience and persistence and more than a little courage if we are to succeed in our quest but here, in this final hour of our ignominious history, there has never been a time when the teachings of the wise have been more desperately needed, so our attempt to become enlightened has to be worth the effort.

What is Truth?

A wise person once said: "You shall know the truth and the truth shall make you free". (John 8:32). That's probably as good a description as any of 'spiritual enlightenment': that moment when we get to discover for ourselves what that truth actually is.

So before we go on, let's have a think about truth.

If I tell the truth, what I am doing is being honest about what I believe to be true at this particular instant in time. If my understanding of the truth changes tomorrow in the light of new information, that doesn't mean I am lying now. I'm perhaps just, temporarily and unwittingly, badly informed or delusional.

In this crazy age of 'fake news', it can be hard to know where the truth lies, since even the 'sworn truth' so often turns out to be lies and even some of the most powerful people in the world appear to be delusional.

So when we say that something is 'true', what do we really mean?

Supposing I strike a match, it ignites and I put my finger in the flame: what will happen?

When I ask this question to groups, they immediately respond: "You'd burn yourself!"

So I ask them: "How do you know?"

The discussion arising from this question normally lasts a long time.

Let's look at why.

Isn't it obvious that I will burn myself? How would I know that, if I'd never burned myself before?

Do I believe you if you tell me that I will burn myself? Can I trust you to be honest with me? And in any case, isn't honesty just giving an accurate account of what you believe to be true for you at this moment? And might your belief be subject to change - perhaps if you found out that I had just invented heat-free matches?

Should I just accept what you say, founded either on blind faith or as a kind of insurance policy since, whether I believe you or not, I don't want to take the risk that you might be right.

Suppose I then strike the match and burn myself.

Now maybe I believe you.

But maybe you hypnotised me into feeling the pain, and the blister on my finger is some kind of hallucination. I can continue with my belief, but do I know it to be true?

Supposing I burn myself on several occasions, sometimes when you're not around to hypnotise me. Could the pain and discolouration still be an implanted suggestion you left me with? (Sadly, my fingers are looking a bit rough at this stage and I'm taking lots of aspirin and running out of bandages, so my doubt is starting to waver a bit!)

Supposing you introduce me to lots of other people who all agree that they have burned themselves on matches in the past and are certain that this is an inevitable consequence of putting fingers in flames.

Supposing I read scientific journals which describe the laws of heat transfer, supported by mathematical proofs and backed up by countless examples of experimental evidence to support the theory that naked flame has a detrimental effect on human skin tissue.

Supposing I read in magazines, or I hear on the news, that putting fingers in flames is not recommended for my well-being and the government is thinking of bringing in a new law to prevent people from messing about with matches and, in any case, there's a health and safety warning on the box!

Supposing my religious leader, assuming I had one, tells me that it says in "The Book" that I must not mess about with matches because the almighty deity will ensure that bad stuff will happen to me after I die if I do. I won't get to go to paradise and be bathed in golden light; I won't be loved unconditionally and, incidentally, I will burn myself if I am daft enough to stick my finger in a naked flame.

OK so, assuming that I was actually awake and not dreaming (and assuming that I could even begin to know that), I'd probably have to be a bit silly not to believe that there was something in this by now, wouldn't I? But would I really know?

Had I been reluctant, at first, to take your word for it, there were several heavyweight reasons given above that might have convinced me to believe you:

Consensus - lots of people say so.

Scientific evidence - scientists have used mathematical reasoning to suggest that touching a lighted match would probably hurt; experiments in different parts of the world across thousands of years have yielded similar results and, so far, no one has been able to disprove this hypothesis. In other words, it is potentially falsifiable but not yet falsified, so it's probably true and we might as well take it as read until someone comes up with a better idea.

Authority - the guys with the power say it's bad for me and it says so in my magazine, and in a bestselling book and even on the BBC! And of course if religious leaders tell me it's true then who am I to argue with Big G?

Experience - I've felt it for myself.

Which is the most convincing?

Consensus or science perhaps? Then again, there was a time when a majority of people believed that the Earth was flat, and it's not that long since a majority of people, including some eminent scientists at the time, believed that the sun went round the Earth. Well, it was obvious, wasn't it? Then the next bunch of scientists proved them wrong. So, can we trust scientists to know everything about everything yet? Well, maybe not everything, though they are very clever and they do know lots of stuff, so I might be kind of inclined to go with what they say about most things, since I don't have a good enough grasp of mathematics to have the temerity to argue with them.

Of course, if they ever get to the point where they think they know everything, scientific method will be thrown out with the last test tube and we will stagnate in our complacency. If life is like a computer game, we will need to keep progressing to new levels, otherwise it will be 'game over' and time to go out and buy new software.

Who do we trust to tell us the truth then? Are magazine articles and books always written by people who know what they are talking about? Do editors vet them all to make sure that no rubbish gets into print? Does peer review always get done by peers with infallible judgement? Do governments always know what's best for us? Or teachers? Or judges? Or New Age gurus? Or that guy behind the bar down the road? And do all the 'holy ones' among us really have a direct line to the Almighty?

Personal experience, maybe, has the edge when we are talking about verifying what is or isn't true but can we always be sure that what we experience is true? Who's truth are we talking about anyway?

And when it comes to issues other than our little example about matches, are we always so sure and is our certainty justified? If we serve on a jury or vote in an election or referendum, are we always fully aware of the potential consequences and absolutely convinced that we made the right decision? If the 'ultimate truth' about life, the universe and everything jumps up, slaps us in the face and yells: "Here I am!", how will we know it's not just a product of our own wishful thinking?

We can't dismiss something as untrue just because we find it difficult to understand or it's not very interesting, and we can't claim something is true just because it fits in with what we already believe and doesn't seem to conflict with anything we think we already know.

"People often seek to arrive at conclusions which gratify their implanted prejudices and satisfy inherited bias. They accept no facts in an argument save those that dovetail into their existing outlook. If one judges every fact by the standards of one's earlier experience alone, one prevents new knowledge from arising."

Dr. Paul Brunton

Most scientists readily admit that our knowledge of the universe is incomplete. We test our theories and work out the laws as far as our observations and reasoning allow us at any given time but the 'truth', as we currently know it, is subject to change in the light of new evidence which broadens or re-clarifies our viewpoint.

My own approach is that, whenever I get too excited about an idea or concept, I scrap it and start over from first principles, checking facts and reasoning and looking at it from all angles. If I reach the same conclusion, I am likely to decide that there may be some truth in it and I explore the implications of that being so, but I try to remain open to any new possibilities that I had not yet considered and that might offer further insights into the truth of the matter, rather than merely confirming my own pre-existing opinions.

If my "truth" turns out to be inaccurate, the question then becomes: was there an objective truth all along that I just wasn't aware of at the time or is truth an ephemeral thing that depends on our individual perceptions of what is real? Is there any such thing as 'ultimate truth', beyond all doubt and contradiction for all time?

Philosophers have asked these questions and argued about the answers, possibly for as long as there have been philosophers. What do you think?

35

What is Reality?

The challenge we face when we try to answer this question is that most of us think we already know what reality is. It's just common sense isn't it? Or so it seemed until scientists came along and started to pick apart some of the strands of the tapestry we had constructed. We appear to be the most highly evolved species we know of. We can go wherever we like and do whatever we please on land, sea and air and we are already expanding our horizons off-world, out beyond our moon, towards the nearest planets and asteroids. Yet we are still very limited creatures because our five senses can only extend so far towards the very large or the very small.

Even with our vision augmented by powerful telescopes and microscopes, there are limits beyond which our technology can no longer help us. We can see trillions of galaxies, containing more stars than there are grains of sand on our planet, and yet we can only see as far as the light travelling across space has already come; beyond that, we are left guessing. We have glimpsed the subatomic particles that make up the visible parts of our universe, from suns and planets to our own bodies, yet we are struggling to look any further because there is a point of smallness beyond which our efforts to look completely mess up whatever it is that we are trying to look at.

Perhaps we will find ways to overcome these difficulties but, for the moment, only the mind can go beyond these limits. In our attempts to understand reality, we make educated guesses that suggest to us that there is other stuff billions of times smaller than the stuff we know about while, beyond the massive patch of universe we can see, there may be more of the same stretching on to infinity or there may be nothing, or there may even be other universes alongside our own, like bubbles floating around in we know not what.

Despite all the unknowns beyond the limits of our perception, we have learned a lot about the bits that we are able to look at more closely, and by doing so we have discovered that a 'common sense' view of reality just doesn't hold up any more. Over the past century, the scientists among us have realised that even time and space are not at all what we have always thought they were. Their findings are mind-blowing and intriguing, as we are about to see in the next chapter, and that's just the science!

In addition to the new knowledge that science has provided access to, there is the wealth of knowledge gained through direct experience by wise men and women across millennia. We could, of course, scrap all that stuff and call it 'unscientific' but what a wasted resource that would be! Since all knowledge is acquired through the perceptions of human beings, we perhaps need to acknowledge that there are various ways of using the instrument we call our brain and see what we can learn via these various methods rather than risk throwing out any babies with the bathwater.

If we assume, for the purposes of what follows, that a scientific approach and so-called 'mystical' approaches are not mutually exclusive, we may find that there are common threads in what each has to offer, which, perhaps, is only to be expected if both are looking at the same thing – reality – from different viewpoints. The search for an overarching view of reality that considers evidence from all relevant sources takes us into the realm of philosophy.

What is Philosophy?

Philosophy can be thought of as our search for truth: for knowledge that is independent of personal opinion. Philosophers use a variety of methods to find out what is true about anything, beginning with what we know, something indisputable, which they call a 'premise'. For example, the premise: 'a triangle has three sides' is not something we would argue with since the definition of a triangle is a two-dimensional shape with three sides. Once we have our premise, we can use it as a foundation for logical, reasoned arguments in our efforts to extend our knowledge and deepen our understanding of our world.

New knowledge allows us to change our thoughts, which in turn can change our character and our actions; our actions affect other people as well as ourselves so, by changing our minds, we can change our lives and, potentially, change the world. With new knowledge comes new responsibility and philosophers therefore seek not only knowledge as information and experience but the wisdom to use it well for the benefit of mankind.

> *"Genuine philosophy shows men how to live!"*

> *Dr. Paul Brunton*

To be a philosopher, all our preconceptions and prejudices must be cast aside. Our studies, whether from books or with a teacher, must be to gain new knowledge and discover what is true, not to confirm or endorse our own beliefs, otherwise we can end up by seeing things that do not exist outside our own imagination.

> *"The kernel of the scientific outlook is the refusal to regard one's own desires, tastes and interests as affording a key to the understanding of the world."*

> *Bertrand Russell, 1913*

Like all good philosophers, scientists also use careful reasoning, making every attempt to eliminate bias and scrutinising all available evidence, but while philosophers can engage in circular arguments for centuries, or agree that various viewpoints are equally valid, scientists are mostly concerned with what can be measured. Many things that interest philosophers, such as our sense of values, creativity and 'spiritual matters', are outside the scope of science.

What is Science?

> *"In science it often happens that scientists say, 'You know that's a really good argument; my position is mistaken,' and then they would actually change their minds and you never hear that old view from them again. They really do it. It doesn't happen as often as it should, because scientists are human and change is sometimes painful. But it happens every day. I cannot recall the last time something like that happened in politics or religion."*

> *Carl Sagan*

Science is not a belief system; it is a method of enquiry. It used to be called 'natural philosophy', since it was a branch of philosophy that specialised in looking at the natural physical world. Although the scientific method that we value so highly today is a fairly new development in the West, it has been practiced for centuries in some Eastern cultures.

What separates modern scientific method from our past efforts to understand our world is that although, like philosophers, we start with our observations and the stuff we are already pretty sure we know, which scientists call 'axioms', and use logic and reasoning to work out what we think is going on, we then go several steps further.

First, we try to predict what the consequences would be in the real world if our ideas, or 'hypotheses', were true. Then we use experiments to test them in every way we can, not in an attempt to prove them to be true but in an attempt to disprove them and show them to be false, if possible. The observed results of such experiments need to be measurable, repeatable by others and, preferably, have some kind of mathematical proofs to back them up. If the hypotheses stand up to this kind of scrutiny for any length of time, we have a working 'theory' that moves us on a bit further in our attempt to understand reality. At any point, the theory is open to further scrutiny and if anyone comes up with evidence that it is wrong, the whole thing is scrapped and it's back to the drawing board for the entire global scientific community: even the guys who got the Nobel Prize for coming up with the theory in the first place.

Scientists are always open to this kind of paradigm shift and don't take it personally if anyone has the temerity to demolish their ideas. When Newton's view of the world was shaken to its foundations by people like Einstein, with his relativity theories, or Bohr and Heisenberg, with their discovery of quantum physics, the shock waves that rippled through the scientific edifice were profound, but the paradigm shifts they brought about were fairly rapidly embraced and used to bring about huge advances in our knowledge and technology. This is likely to happen again in the future, as wider theories either contradict or embrace our current notions, so we need to be very careful when we talk about any kind of 'fully objective reality'.

In contrast, 'pseudoscientists' or 'fundamentalists' may become so attached to their way of seeing the world that they will do anything to hold onto it, even if that means ignoring clear evidence to the contrary or inventing increasingly weird concepts to defend it. I'm not about to come up with a list of some of the strange ideas included in the latter category. You can probably think of your own examples, just by using the above criteria. Anything that constantly needs to be justified by increasingly absurd or irrational explanations is likely to be deserving of a place on your list.

You can also use this as a yardstick to check the content of this book as you go along, in order to make sure that we don't stray into exotic realms that could be dismissed as 'pseudoscience', 'happy clappy hippy stuff', 'esoteric nonsense', ' superstition' or plain old 'wishful thinking'.

We will try to remain grounded in science as far as possible but to confine ourselves exclusively to science would not be helpful. The idea that anything that has not been proved by science, or is outside its remit, is either false or insignificant may, in itself, be a philosophical assumption based on prejudice.

For all its strengths and value to us as a species, science can also limit us, since it may generate a materialistic view of the world that can narrow our view and lead to reductionism and even nihilism, where everything is seen as a pointless accident, without meaning. This may be an idea that some people are comfortable with but, for others, it may lead to depression and even suicide, since a pointless world may appear to offer nothing to live for, let alone any reason for making a collective effort to save it.

At the other extreme, there may be people who have no interest at all in science and have a deep conviction that they occupy a moral high ground, but then devolve any kind of responsibility for saving the world to a higher power, due to a belief that a supreme being will intervene, eventually, if things get really bad. According to this kind of reasoning, whatever happens is the divine will of the Almighty and if every species of life on Earth were to be extinguished tomorrow, it would be because the supreme deity was angry with us and we probably deserved it and anyway the good among us would be rewarded in heaven so, unless we have done bad stuff in this lifetime, why worry?

Between these two fairly unhelpful approaches, we are left with those of us who, irrespective of what we think about science, religion or philosophy, feel at a gut level that all living creatures are important and inherently worth saving. The fact that you are reading this book gives me hope that you are one of these people and that you are open to the possibility that, by just shifting our collective world-view very slightly, we might be able to learn to get on well enough with each other to find solutions to our problems. It may also have occurred to you, as it has to me, that, if we are to survive as a species, we need not only to understand our world and our place within it, but also to take responsibility for what we do to it and for how we treat each other. To bring about the required enlightening shift in our perception, we will need to consider the very best that science, philosophy and religion can offer.

Across the millennia, there have been wise people who have searched for answers to all the questions that currently perplex scientists and philosophers alike. Their approach may have been slightly different to our modern scientific method, since everything fell under their scrutiny and they lacked the kind of equipment that we have available nowadays but, in many cases, their reasoning appears to have been sound.

For example, the Tibetan Buddhists had a thing called a 'principle of negation' which basically says that just because you look for something and haven't managed to find it yet, that doesn't mean that it doesn't exist. As criminologists would say: "absence of evidence is not evidence of absence." Without the use of microscopes, we could claim that it's impossible to prove that anything smaller than we can see with our naked eye actually exists, so we might as well assume that it doesn't, thereby discounting the presence of microscopic life forms from amoebae, bacteria, archaea and viruses to the cells of our own body. Fortunately, we do have microscopes and this whole realm of reality has been opened up for us to study, just as the larger universe has been opened up by the invention of the telescope and the ability to measure different parts of the electromagnetic spectrum beyond what is visible to the naked eye, including infra-red and ultraviolet light, X-rays, radio waves and gamma radiation. Even without these inventions, the Tibetan Buddhists managed to work out, by reasoning alone, that matter consisted of atoms and that time was relative, centuries before Einstein, Bohr and Rutherford were even born.

'That which is not yet proved' is not the same as 'that which is not possible'. When scientists decide not to follow a particular line of enquiry because it is not falsifiable, they may shut it down prematurely. At the moment, for example, we have ideas that we cannot test one way or the other because we not only lack the equipment we would need to falsify them, we may never be able to develop such equipment. We can't go outside our own universe to prove or disprove the 'multiverse' theory, or delve to scales billions of times smaller than an atom to explore what is going on within the tiniest regions of the fabric of spacetime, at a scale that we call the Planck length, but does that mean that we should give up?

Some scientists would say we should but others continue to develop their ideas about what lies beyond the current limits, using mathematical reasoning to predict what may or may not be there. This can be a very productive method and has led to discoveries such as the Higgs boson, the existence of which was predicted mathematically long before it was confirmed by building the massive particle accelerator at CERN in Geneva, Switzerland. Other old ideas were abandoned long ago. For example, the wave nature of light seemed to suggest a medium that was waving, referred to as 'The Ether', but this was rejected, not because its existence was disproved but because the maths worked perfectly without it and so did not require it to exist! Whether we were correct in making that decision remains to be seen.

Even for those theoretical physicists who stand at the very frontiers of science and look for answers far beyond our current capacity to prove or disprove them, there are realms of inquiry into which most are reluctant to go, not least of which is the field of research into human consciousness, though this situation, as we shall see, is changing.

An extreme idea that most would be unlikely to consider worthy of their efforts to embrace as a potential line of scientific enquiry is the concept of a 'conscious' universe, and yet, in our quest to get at the truth, we really can't afford to dismiss even this idea without considering any available evidence.

Before we get to that, however, we need to ask ourselves: does such a thing as spiritual enlightenment even exist and, if so, how do we get it? When those who claim to have reached such a state speak of the 'paths' that took them there, what exactly are they talking about?

What are Paths?

People have been seeking truth for millennia and many have spoken about various 'spiritual paths' or routes that can take us to the mysterious state of 'enlightenment'. Some have also said that there is no need to rush in these matters. There is a story somewhere of a seeker who is told by a passing sage that he will become enlightened one day, when he has lived as many lifetimes as there are leaves on a rather large nearby tree.

Well, that was probably a good story at the time it was told, when the Earth and humanity were young and the future seemed to stretch ahead indefinitely. Now, however, we have reached a point where the continued survival of our species, and even all life on Earth, may depend on our collective enlightenment during this current lifetime, rather than leaving the job of working it out to our grandchildren or to any would-be reincarnated future selves.

44

To facilitate this process, we are about to take a look at what others have told us. However, it won't be a matter of taking anyone's word for it: the aim of our current line of inquiry into the truth is that we will come to see it for ourselves.

Throughout history, our fellow seekers after truth, wherever they happened to live in this world, have always seen that there are several essential ingredients on their various 'paths'. These key ingredients include knowledge, meditation and service.

Don't worry though, nobody is suggesting that, to become enlightened, you should go out and earn yourself a degree in physics, or a sainthood, or shut yourself away in a cave for several years while you contemplate your navel - unless of course you want to do any or all of those things. We will, however, investigate some hows and whys of meditation and service and consider some of the knowledge that is available to us from various sources, from up-to-the-minute scientific insights to old-as-the-hills wisdom from ancient masters.

It has also been said that, to embark on any kind of spiritual path, we have to work on ourselves somehow; that we are imperfect and need to perfect ourselves; that we need to elevate our level of consciousness or achieve some mysterious and elusive goal.

Don't let that put you off! You do not need to try to magically transform yourself into some kind of perfect person. Although, ultimately, it may be said that we are all one, you are, nevertheless, living this life through a particular instrument, a unique expression of the universal through the individual, and that individual is perfectly suited to its role. In an orchestra, if a flute were to suddenly wake up to the universality of music, it wouldn't be helpful for it to start trying to sound like a tuba!

Although you may find that qualities such as kindness and compassion become more important to you as your sense of connectedness increases, and the very idea of harming or exploiting other people will probably become as inconceivable as the idea of cutting off your own leg, any ideas that suggest that we are not 'good enough' to even embark upon this quest are unhelpful and can prevent us from simply being aware of being, right here, right now and noticing what we already are.

This book sets out some of the ways that we can remind ourselves of this simple concept and come to know it both intellectually and as our own direct experience. On the way, we will consider the insights of those who have walked this way before us, from scientists to sages, and see what they can offer us to help us on our journey.

"You wander from room to room, hunting for the diamond necklace that is already around your neck!"

Rumi

Part 1 - What Do We Already Know?

The efforts of human beings to figure out what the truth is about life, the universe and everything have taken them down many different paths. You might think that, if the truth is the truth, they would all, eventually, come to the same conclusions, whatever path they took. In the case of 'ultimate truth', if there is such a thing, perhaps that should be so but, until we get to that point, it will always be a matter of: "who's truth is it and what kind of truth are we talking about and does that truth change or look different from where we happen to be standing?"

As we have seen, the various methods we have used in our hunt for the truth include science and philosophy. While it's true that philosophy alone would not have got us to the moon or given us television, air travel, satnavs or the internet, the human mind is also capable of going beyond the limits of what our measuring equipment is able to reach, and our ability to ask "what lies beyond that then?" has prompted us to do the science that has brought us to our present state of understanding of our world. So we will start with what science can tell us, so far, about what we are and what reality appears to be.

If science was not your favourite subject at school, or you never had the opportunity to study it, please don't let that put you off. As many people before me have said, we are the universe looking at itself, and I believe that anything we discover about how it works should be shared with all those members of the human race who are interested in such matters, in language that everyone can understand, so that we can all engage in intelligent debate about the possible implications of such findings.

Some scientists, of course, from Carl Sagan and Patrick Moore to Brian Greene, Bill Nye and Brian Cox, have been doing a great job of making science accessible to everyone and I am optimistic that it is possible for productive communication to take place between philosophers, scientists, politicians, the general public and those who subscribe to various faiths, despite the obstacles that lead to many people on the planet remaining oblivious to the workings of the cosmos.

Quite apart from the lack of availability of a scientific education in many parts of the world, a substantial number of people are fully occupied with the day to day tasks of survival, such as getting enough food and water or avoiding being murdered. Even for those with adequate resources and the leisure to contemplate such matters, some of the stuff we have found out so far is so mind-blowing and weird that it is difficult even for scientists themselves to take it all in! Although modern society has a tendency to view guys in white lab coats as all-knowing, scientists themselves know that this is far from true. As many of them have said, if you think you understand quantum physics or you know what goes on inside a black hole, you are probably wrong, but that doesn't mean that we should stop trying.

So, whoever you are, and whatever your educational background, you are welcome to participate in this current debate and you won't need a degree in physics or mathematics to follow the topics covered in this chapter. You will not find yourself being patronised or left behind. It is my hope that this might go some way towards narrowing, and perhaps bridging, the yawning chasm that currently separates substantial chunks of the global community from the lofty towers of science and indeed seems to help to drive some of us, including certain world leaders, back into the dark ages; with superstition and blind faith taking the place of scientific knowledge or even basic common sense.

Science is neither good nor bad. In theory, scientists are morally neutral: it is the use we make of their findings to inform our technology that can be helpful or unhelpful. Our insights into the atomic nucleus, for example, led to nuclear weapons on the one hand and the radioisotopes used in hospitals to save countless lives on the other. Whether or not we feel that scientists should be held accountable for the potential use or misuse of their discoveries, any decisions to use or misuse their findings are largely beyond their control, tending to be based more on politics and profitability than altruism or necessity, and ignoring the warnings of the entire scientific community seems to be a tactic of choice for the committed megalomaniac.

If you are already an expert in any of these fields, my approach may seem overly simplistic. You are welcome to correct me if you disagree with anything I say and you might want to skip lightly through some or all of what follows, though, since none of us can be experts at everything, it might still be useful to follow this thread and see where it leads.

If, on the other hand, lots of the stuff we are about to discuss is new to you or is too mind-boggling to get your head around in one sitting, you might prefer to come at it one chunk at a time. I am not, for one moment, suggesting that you need to know all of this: it's just a summary of the information and ideas that I have found interesting and believe to be relevant to our current search. So if, at any point, you start to get a bit bogged down, especially in the science bits, you can always jump on to the next section, and maybe return to it later if you want to. There's no maths involved and there's no test at the end of it so just sit back and enjoy this voyage of discovery into the fabric of reality.

Chapter 1 - What Science is Telling Us

"What we observe as material bodies and forces are nothing but shapes and variations in the structure of space."

Erwin Schrödinger

As a foundation for our quest, we need to have some idea of what we mean when we talk about our universe and our own bodies. It could be said that one of the most important reasons for having an education, even more than to learn how to read and write or do mathematics, is to gain a more accurate idea of what we are made of than our eyes alone can tell us. Given that we spend a great deal of time judging each other on the basis of the external appearance of our bodies, it can be a revelation to discover that the differences we may consider to be so important are superficial. The colour of our skin is simply a variation in how much pigment we produce to protect ourselves from the sun, while our facial characteristics, the size and shape of our bodies and even our gender are insignificant when we take a microscope and have a closer look at what our seemingly different bodies are made of.

"This oak tree and me, we're made of the same stuff."

Carl Sagan

News from the Biology Department

Just as houses can be built from individual bricks, our bodies are made of cells – tiny blobs of jelly that are a bit like frog spawn but so small that we can't see them without a microscope. They come in various types, depending on where they are in our bodies and what jobs they have to do. There are long thin ones that are able to contract and expand and form the muscles that allow our bodies to move, and there are even longer, thinner nerve cells that can transmit signals around our bodies like the wires in electrical circuits. There are liver cells, heart cells, brain cells, skin cells and blood cells - all specialised to play their particular roles in keeping us alive and healthy and helping us to reproduce so that the human race continues on into the future.

Although all of these cells look different, we need all of them working together to make a fully-functioning human, just as we need a diverse range of people working to their own strengths and capabilities to make a fully functional society and we need all aspects of nature working together to keep the living skin of our planet, our biosphere, alive.

As well as showing us the importance of diversity in contributing to our overall unity and survival, our studies of biology have revealed even greater wonders. All of those specialised cells, not only in our own bodies but in those of all animals and plants too, have underlying similarities. All of them, except red blood cells, have a nucleus in the middle which contains DNA. If we think of a cell as a kind of factory, then the nucleus is where it stores the huge blueprint, like a master recipe book with instructions for everything from how to build the factory itself to what overall purpose it serves and how to make all the tools required for the jobs that need doing.

The recipe, or the genetic code, can be used as a template to make all the machinery of the factory and all its products. The factory itself is quite awesome. It is made of a kind of jelly, called cytoplasm, wrapped up in a membrane that's a bit like a double layer of oil on water. The jelly contains a kind of scaffolding made out of thin filaments and among this there are powerhouses called mitochondria and strings of things called ribosomes which act like an assembly line to build chains of amino acids and fold them into proteins, such as enzymes and hormones, which do important jobs in the cell and in the body generally.

As a biochemist and cell physiologist, I could spend the rest of this book quite happily telling you all about the mind-bogglingly awesome stuff that goes on in cells but we need to move on if we are to plumb the deepest depths of reality. If you want to have your mind boggled a bit more, you might like to look on YouTube at some of the fabulous animations, such as Harvard University's *The Inner Life of the Cell*, that show you what is going on inside you right now, in the millions of cells that are working round the clock to keep you alive and well.

Meanwhile, I want to take us deeper still, to look at what these tiny 'factories' and all their contents, equipment and products are actually made of. We already mentioned proteins. Since all the machines trundling away inside our cells are made out of these things, it's easy to see why they are an essential component of a healthy diet. When we eat proteins, our digestive system breaks them down into amino acids, like breaking the string of a beaded necklace, and ships them into the various cells so that they can be reassembled into whatever new proteins are needed there. It's a bit like when we send our old cars or washing machines to be stripped down into their individual parts and recycled into TV monitors, phones and refrigerators. In the body, that bit of meat or tofu you had for lunch will soon be recycled into various new proteins, from the insulin you need to regulate your blood sugar to the interferon that helps you to fight off the flu.

Incidentally, a virus, you may be interested to know, is a bit like an alien spacecraft that can take over the factory by introducing a new bit of code that gets all the machinery to stop making TVs and fridges and start churning out copies of itself instead, until the factory finally explodes and all the newly-made viruses go off to invade other cells. Hacking is nothing new: it's always been a thing!

Two other very important constituents of our diet include carbohydrates and fats, and these are broken down and reassembled in the body as well. Carbohydrates, like starch, are broken down into simple sugars, like glucose, that can be used as fuel to give us the energy we need to power the 'factories'. Fats, or lipids, are broken down into fatty acids and glycerol, which can be reassembled into cell membranes and have various other important roles to play. Of course, since our bodies are largely made of water, and because all of these molecules need a fluid environment to move around in, we have to drink plenty too.

All of these substances – fats, proteins, carbohydrates and water – are molecules, which in turn are constructed from atoms. Just as millions of written words can be built from an alphabet containing just a few letters or symbols, millions of different types of molecules can be made from a hundred or so types of atom, and these are called elements. The molecules that make up our bodies are largely composed of just a few elements: Carbon, Hydrogen, Oxygen, Nitrogen, Phosphorous and Sulphur (CHONPS) with smaller amounts of potassium, calcium, iron, magnesium, zinc and other minerals thrown in. When we start to look more deeply at what these 'elements' are and where they came from, we enter the realms of chemistry and astrophysics.

News from the Chemistry Department

We can go deeper into the fabric of reality than even my own field of biochemistry can take us by considering the basic elements that the entire universe is made from. So far, we have discovered 118 different elements, the existence of the latest four having been confirmed in December 2015. Chemists have spent lifetimes working out the structure of these things and looking at how they interact with each other to form everything from water and the salt we sprinkle on our food to medicines and people.

The elements can be arranged in order of their size and complexity to form a special kind of chart called a periodic table, beginning with the smallest and lightest, hydrogen, and building up towards the largest and heaviest that we are currently aware of. In their purest form, at room temperature, some of these are gases – such as hydrogen, oxygen, nitrogen and neon - or liquids like ammonia or soft solids like sodium and lithium or hard solids such as iron, silver, gold, copper and lead, and some of these can conduct electricity. Chemists look at physical properties, such as the temperatures at which each of these elements will freeze into a solid, melt into a liquid, evaporate into a gas or condense back into a liquid. They also look at how to put them together in various ways to form molecules and whether or not they produce something useful, like water or steel or medicines, or whether they are, literally, an explosive combination.

News from the Astronomy Department

When chemists and astrophysicists put their heads together, they can tell us that all of the main elements that make up our own bodies are at the low end of the periodic table and were made in the hearts of suns like our own. They were released as dust and gas when those stars exploded and then were pulled together by gravity to form the planet Earth. Anything heavier than iron needed much greater temperatures and pressures to shove together lighter elements, and the only sort of place where this kind of thing can occur naturally is inside a massive explosion such as a supernova or a collision between two neutron stars. So if you have a gold, silver or platinum wedding ring, you are looking at the aftermath of one of the most spectacular events in the cosmos! We are indeed, as Carl Sagan used to say, "star-stuff".

News from the Physics Department

Going deeper still into what scientists have to say on the subject of reality, we can begin to explore some of the remarkable insights that have emerged from the field of physics, where explorations so far have given us a whole lot to think about. Any proper quest for 'enlightenment' must surely take these findings into account. Therefore, we are about to take our quest to the limits of the unbelievably small and the mind-bogglingly huge, and into the nature of space and time. We will start with what we know about the finest ingredients of the stuff we call reality.

> *"If you wish to understand the universe, think of energy, frequency and vibration."*
>
> *Nikola Tesla*

Quantum Physics - Matter is not what we think it is

As we have seen above, everything is made of atoms, including our own bodies. So in our attempt to find out what we are, and what reality might be, it could be very helpful to start by asking ourselves what we know, so far, about atoms.

To get some idea of how small an atom is, let's think about how many atoms there are inside a cricket ball (or a baseball). Imagine a cricket ball the size of the planet Earth. On that scale, an atom is the size of a grape. So if you imagine the entire planet packed with grapes, that's about how many atoms there are in a cricket ball!

Think about it for a moment.

If you're struggling to imagine anything so unbelievably tiny, you're not alone! Stay with it though because we're now going to take a look at what those atoms are made of.

In school, you may have been taught that an atom looks a bit like the sun with planets going around it. There's a thing called a nucleus in the middle and things called electrons in orbit around this nucleus. The nucleus is made up of things called protons and neutrons.

For the purposes of learning basic science in school, the little solar system image of an atom holds up quite well, but it's much weirder than that and I have to say that I was a bit mortified when, in later life, I learned that the stuff I'm about to describe had been known to science since the beginning of the twentieth century, yet my teachers had made no attempt to share this crucial information with us, perhaps in the belief that it was too complex and weird for the teenage brain to wrap itself around. However, discovering this information is potentially life-changing and I believe it is the birth-right of every person on the planet to be informed about what we have learned so far, because atoms are what we are all made of, and so is the planet we live on, the food we eat and every star in the sky.

So what's so special about atoms? Well, let's take a look at the smallest atom, a hydrogen atom, which has only one proton in its nucleus and one electron in orbit around it. If you imagine a hydrogen atom the size of a seven storey building, or the dome of St. Paul's cathedral, then on that scale the nucleus in the middle is the size of a grain of salt.

The electron whizzing round it is about two thousand times smaller than that!

If you have not heard about this before, just take a few moments to absorb that information. Another way of looking at it is to imagine an atom the size of a football stadium. On that scale, the nucleus would be the size of a marble sitting in the middle of the pitch and the electron would be about the size of a poppy seed.

What we're saying here is that atoms are almost entirely empty space! The only reason we are not currently falling through the floor is because of electromagnetic fields which prevent our atoms from passing through those of other substances, such as floors, in much the same way that like poles of magnets repel each other.

The electron itself is whizzing around so fast that it seems to occupy the whole space, like a rotating helicopter blade appearing as a disc. It's going so fast that we can't know its position without stopping it and if we measure its speed we can't know where it is because it's not in any one place long enough. This is called Heisenberg's uncertainty principle. All we can know about an electron is the probability of it being in a particular place at any given time.

Actually, the uncertainty principle is not so much a result of electrons and other particles behaving in strange ways; it has more to do with our difficulty in knowing what they are up to, strange or not. That's because, to see something, you have to shine light on it and the light has to bounce back to your eye or your measuring equipment. Because sub-atomic particles are so small, firing a photon of light at them interferes with what they are doing so you can't really say what they were up to before you tried to look at them and messed everything up. Scientists call this the measurement problem because you can't measure what is going on without interfering with what you are measuring.

So we have kind of reached a limit to how small we can go with our looking at things at the moment. That doesn't mean that the subatomic particles we know about are the smallest things that exist - we think that there are things billions of times smaller, perhaps little vibrating strings or loops at a scale we call the Planck length - but we have to infer their existence from our mathematics until we work out how to go about looking at anything that tiny.

"Every sub-atomic interaction consists of the annihilation of the original particles and the creation of new subatomic particles. The subatomic world is a continual dance of creation and annihilation, of mass changing into energy and energy changing into mass. Transient forms sparkle in and out of existence, creating a never-ending, forever newly created reality."

Gary Zukov, The Dancing Wu Li Masters

Particles, waves and "wavicles"

All that would be strange enough if we actually knew what an electron is. But we don't really.

There have been countless experiments carried out during the past century which have tried to find out whether an electron is a particle or a wave of energy. A single tiny particle, such as an electron, can pass through either one slit in a piece of metal (as a particle would be expected to do) or through two slits at the same time, causing an interference pattern on a screen (as a wave would be expected to do). It turns out that an electron can behave as either a particle or a wave, depending on what the scientist conducting the experiment is looking for! Photons of light do this too.

Now again, think about the implications of this. It seems to suggest that what goes on inside the atoms that make up our universe can be influenced by the mere presence of an observer.

So, you may rightly ask, if the electron is so insubstantial, what is it that gives the material world its hard substance? Is it the proton in the middle of an atom that is a solid particle?

Well, actually, no. The nucleus of an atom is made up of protons and neutrons, and these, disconcertingly, can behave as particles or waves, just as electrons do.

Protons and neutrons are made of even smaller things called quarks and gluons, which are held together by forces a billion billion billion times greater than the pressure at the deepest depths of the sea, yet they are no more substantial than electrons. And they don't just sit there quietly while their cloud of electrons buzzes around them like a swarm of demented bees, they whizz around themselves at close to the speed of light, where our ordinary notions of time break down.

What's even weirder still is that, in the world of particle physics, these basic elementary particles can flit in and out of existence in fractions of a second and can transform into different things. Matter and energy are interchangeable so lots of energy of motion can form a particle, as if out of nothing, and particles can break down into energy.

"Continually emerging, it returns again and again to nothingness."

Lao Tse

This is a lot to take in, so do take a moment to go and have a cup of tea if you want to because we're just getting started. Perhaps the weirdest thing we have learned about the sub-atomic world is a phenomenon called non-locality.

Non-locality and Entanglement

Electrons move around the nucleus of an atom in discrete shells or orbitals. Moving from an inside shell to one further out requires energy, and falling back to an inner shell gives off energy. The energy is released or absorbed in discrete packets called 'quanta', which is why we call this 'quantum mechanics'. Absorbing a quantum of energy allows an electron to jump up to the next shell outwards, while dropping down a level gives off a quantum of energy (a photon).

So far so good, but here's where it gets really creepy. When an electron switches from one orbital to another, it doesn't travel there, it just instantaneously stops being in the one it was in and appears in the other one.

Before it makes this 'quantum leap', it appears to smear itself out over a large region of spacetime before collapsing back into its chosen orbital. This would be like, for example, the planet Mars smearing itself out across the galaxy and then disappearing from its own place in the solar system and immediately popping up in the orbit of Jupiter. Thankfully, large things like planets don't behave the same way that particles do in the sub-atomic world!

Now electrons, apparently, like to go around in pairs. They have a quality which physicists have called 'spin' and in any pair of electrons, one spins one way while the other spins the opposite way. Scientists have managed to separate pairs of electrons and put large distances between them. Once they have been separated, if the spin of one of the electrons is deliberately changed, the spin of the other immediately reverses as well. By 'immediately', I mean in no time at all! There is no time for any physical message to be passed through space from one to the other. It's instantaneous.

It's called quantum entanglement, and it always seems to work, however much space there is between the two particles so, in theory, an electron on one side of the universe would be instantly affected by a change in its partner on the other side of the universe. And it's not just electrons that can be entangled in this way, photons of light do it too and so do molecules, even ones that are big enough to be seen under a microscope. Einstein called this "spooky action at a distance". We don't know how it works, but we know it happens and quite a bit of modern technology exists because of it, including the encryption of our bank details on computers.

To help us to grasp this idea of non-locality, we can journey to the imaginary world of Flatland, where the inhabitants are only aware of two dimensions. If that world happened to be a sheet of paper upon which these two-dimensional creatures crawled and we stuck a pen through the paper, we can perhaps imagine the confusion that would cause among the Flatlanders as they tried to explain why they had to keep going around that mysterious area with its invisible forces that prevented them from passing thought it.

Maybe non-locality is not terribly mysterious. Maybe it is just that our limited viewpoint prevents us from seeing an extra dimension. We know that spacetime curves around heavy objects, like a blanket when you roll a ball over it. That's how Einstein explained gravity. We also believe that it can fold back on itself so that things can pass from one layer to the next, via 'wormholes', rather than taking the time to go all the way around.

Now imagine a balloon with a dot on each side and a piece of thread connecting the dots through the interior of the balloon. Pulling on the dot on one side of the balloon would immediately affect the dot on the other side, though to an observer who was unaware of the piece of thread, it would look like magic, because there was no time for one dot to send a signal to the other around the surface of the balloon. Maybe the universe is a bit like that, we just can't see that other dimension.

If your mind is not yet sufficiently boggled and you want to hear something even weirder than that, then the whole thing about the quantum Cheshire Cat might be worthy of your consideration. Scientists have managed to create a piece of equipment through which you fire a particle. The set-up has two channels. In one channel, there is a device that measures mass; in the other, there is a device that measures spin. Now, wait for it, when you fire your particle through this piece of equipment, its spin goes through one channel and its mass goes through the other! Just like the Cheshire Cat in Alice in Wonderland, who had a smile that could detach itself from his face, spin seems to be detachable from the particle and meets up with it again when it completes its journey through the equipment. It's a bit like you going along a corridor in an airport while your personality goes down another one and then getting it back from the luggage turntable before you leave. Spin, then, isn't what we mean when we look at a rotating football; it's far more mysterious than that.

The upshot of all of this is that we don't fully understand what matter is. It's certainly a lot stranger than it appears at face value. Until recently, we didn't even have a good theory to explain why anything has mass. Then a guy called Peter Higgs suggested that matter has mass due to its interactions with a field called the Higgs Field, composed of particles called Higgs bosons. Scientists from several countries spent billions constructing the Large Hadron Collider to test this hypothesis and the Higgs Boson was, eventually, found.

When you really start to think about all of the above, the universe becomes a very strange and fascinating place. What appears substantial and predictable becomes more of a sea of energy, vibrations and possibilities. Particles seem to be elusive clouds of probability which only collapse into something we can measure when an observer looks at them. So, in theory, it's possible that the whole universe is only there when someone is looking at it. Makes you think, doesn't it?

In the words of a guy called George Berkeley: "To be is to be perceived."

The early 20th century poet and priest, Ronald Knox, made this suggestion:

"There was a young man who said 'God
Must find it exceedingly odd
To think that the tree
Should continue to be
When there's no one about in the quad.'
Reply:
'Dear Sir: Your astonishment's odd;
I am always about in the quad.
And that's why the tree
Will continue to be
Since observed by,
Yours faithfully,
God.'"

The disturbing ability of particles to smear themselves out across spacetime and then reappear in one state or another, gave rise to another very famous cat called Schrödinger's cat which, apart from suggesting an obsession of quantum physicists with members of the feline species, helps us to get our heads round the idea of smeariness. In this thought experiment, our hypothetical cat is stuffed inside a box where there is a radioactive source that can, at random, emit a particle that pings a trigger and releases poison gas into the box. While the lid is on the box, there is no way of knowing whether this event has yet taken place, so we can't tell whether the cat is alive or dead until we take the lid off.

Now, to any rational person (who, one assumes, would not treat an animal that way in the first place) the cat is either alive or it is dead. End of. We just get to find out which when we take the lid off. Not so in the quantum world! In the quantum world, the cat is both alive and dead at the same time. The two possibilities are kind of smeared together as a thing called a wave function and are said to be in 'superposition'. When we take the lid off and have a look, we instantly collapse the wave function so that the cat now appears to be in one state or the other. Well, no one has actually done this with a cat yet, but it's what seems to be happening with particles in the quantum realm.

We can take this further and say, "ah but what happens if someone is outside the room and doesn't know what the person inside the room saw?" For this other person, the wave function has not yet collapsed and only does so when he or she enters the room. And what about someone outside the building, or outside the town? And so it goes on until we come to the same kind of conclusion that Richard Knox reached concerning the tree in the quad: nothing in the universe actually exists until it is observed by, well, you know, 'yours faithfully', etcetera.

> *"As a man who has devoted his whole life to the most clear-headed science, to the study of matter, I can tell you as the result of my research about atoms this much: There is no matter as such! All matter originates and exists only by virtue of a force which brings the particles of an atom to vibration and holds this most minute solar system of the atom together...We must assume behind this force the existence of a conscious and intelligent mind. This mind is the matrix of all matter."*

> *Max Planck, Nobel Prize-winning physicist*

If this is your first venture into the strange field of quantum physics, you can be excused for thinking that I am making all this up. It sounds like something from a weird science fiction movie. However, it has been known about for around a century and whole generations of scientists, from Einstein and Bohr to some of the greatest minds of the present day, have been scratching their heads over these phenomena and have tested them inside out and upside down. They have had observers in different rooms and let instruments do the measuring instead of people; they have delayed looking and found the effect can happen across time as well as space, and they have recently come up with an even stranger theory that was reported in *New Scientist* magazine in July 2018.

This new theory suggests that there is a kind of sound or vibration rippling across the universe, forming a sort of mesh that can ping the wave functions of particles that bump into it and cause them to collapse. The idea is that the tiniest particles can pass through the mesh without getting pinged but when a lot of them are held close together to form larger objects, they tend to get pinged a lot so they stick around instead of going back to being smeary wave functions all the time. Assuming that this is so, scientists are now trying to find out how large a particle needs to be before it gets itself pinged. Seriously. They already know that particles ten thousand times bigger than a proton behave in a quantum manner and they are now turning their attention to dust particles.

In summary, quantum physics tells us that matter is not composed of anything solid at all; it is mostly empty space and the basic building blocks that make up everything we see, including our own bodies, are no more substantial than vibrating waves of energy that flicker in and out of existence. These building blocks are only there when we look for them and can communicate with each other instantly, apparently flouting the universal requirement that nothing can travel faster than the speed of light.

So, while we're on the subject, let's have a look at the speed of light.

Relativity - Time is not what we think it is

According to Einstein:

> *The motion of an object through space and the motion of that*
> *object through time always add up to the speed of light.*

Let's think about what that means. If you are standing absolutely still in one place (OK, so that's not actually possible because the Earth is rotating, whizzing round the sun and so on, but if you were not moving through space at all) then all of your movement would be through time.

If you then got into a car and started travelling along a road, some of your movement would now be through space and a bit less of it through time so, for you, time would slow down a bit. At the kind of speeds we can manage on earth, this effect is so small that we don't notice it.

If we were then to climb on board a spaceship and set off through the galaxy at fifty million miles an hour, we might not notice much of a difference but for every two hours that passed, according to the clock on board our ship, three hours would have passed on Earth, because we would be moving so fast that around a third of our motion would be through space and two thirds through time, so our clock would only tick at two thirds the speeds of the ones back on Earth. This gives rise to the famous limerick by Arthur Henry Reginald Butler in Punch, December 1923:

> *"There was a young lady named Bright*
> *Who could travel much faster than light;*
> *She set off one day,*
> *In a relative way,*
> *And came back the previous night."*

and to Science Fiction tales in which space travellers go off-world for a few weeks and come back to find that everyone they knew on Earth has grown old and died during their absence, and they get to meet their great, great, great grandkids!

Science Fiction is difficult to write when you fully grasp this idea. Unless you get around the problem by travelling through wormholes, or have special warp drives or 'singularity drives' that sniff at the limits imposed by the mere fabric of spacetime, Starbase would be long gone by the time you'd boldly been. If you wanted to know how old you were, you would need to wear a personal chronometer and never take it off as you observed the varying rates of life and death in any other creatures you encountered on your travels.

In summary, then, Einstein's theory of relativity tells us that time is not what we think it is but depends on where we are and how fast we are going, and each one of us has a different perception of time.

Let's look at some implications of this.

1. If something could travel as fast as the speed of light, then all its motion would be through space and none of it would be through time, so time would stand still. Well, we know that something does travel at the speed of light. Light travels at the speed of light! So for a photon, time does not exist.

2. Because the fastest speed within the universe is light speed, anything further away than our retinas is unknown to us because its light has not reached us yet. Any object travelling at the speed of light is invisible to an object standing in its path until it reaches it. Therefore we can see nothing beyond our own eyes except the light that has already reached them. (Even then, it takes time for the stimulation of the retina to send signals to the brain and be interpreted as an image.) Anything happening now, further away, remains unknowable since what we see is always light emanating from the

past. We are forever looking back in time at what happened in the past: we can only see the universe as it used to be and have no real way of knowing what is out there right now, even though our telescopes can see right back to the beginning of time.

3. The sub-atomic particles within the atoms that make up everything, including us, travel at fantastic speeds. This means that there may well be discrepancies between our own perception of spacetime and that of the materials we are 'built from'.

"We come spinning out of nothingness
Scattering stars like dust."
Rumi's vision

Seven other very weird things

1. Infinite histories theory suggests that there is just now and that we generate the past by looking backwards in time, while psychologists have found that our memories are unreliable and each one of us has different perceptions of past events, so the past is not necessarily what we think it is.

2. String Theory suggests that the fabric of spacetime consists of tiny strings, loops or membranes or bubbles (quantum froth) that vibrate at different frequencies like violin strings, and it is the particular frequency of vibration which makes one turn out to be an electron and another a quark or other type of 'particle'. We can think of the universe as a kind of cosmic symphony. String theory also suggests that there are possibly eleven dimensions rather than the four we are normally aware of.

3. Loop quantum gravity theorists have come up with the idea that space is composed of tiny loops with a diameter billions of times

smaller than an atomic nucleus, and where these intersect, there are nodes that may be tiny black holes.

4. The black holes we normally read about are massive things that begin as collapsed stars. The gravity inside them is so great that even the space between the nucleus of an atom and its electrons collapses and everything gets squidged together. The gravity can then suck in nearby objects such as planets and other stars, and nothing can escape from it because to do so would mean travelling faster than the speed of light, which is impossible. The boundary between the place where an object could still escape and the place where it would get sucked in forever is called the event horizon. There may be a supermassive black hole at the centre of every galaxy and countless smaller ones elsewhere. The spiralling of a galaxy could be due to its stars being sucked towards the central black hole like water down a plug hole. It is thought that the normal laws of time and space break down inside a black hole. Whether what goes into the hole stays in the hole, or whether it flits through a wormhole and pops up elsewhere, perhaps in the intergalactic voids as dark energy, like a colossal recycling process contributing to the expansion of the universe, is currently unknown but that's my best guess so far.

5. The universe itself is not limited by the laws that exist within it. So although, within the universe, nothing can travel faster than the speed of light, the universe itself can travel much faster than the speed of light! Apparently it did so during the big bang, going from something unimaginably tiny to something infinitely huge in a fraction of a second.

6. Astronomers tell us that we can only see a small fraction of the universe, which may actually be infinite and appears to be expanding. Within this part of the universe that is known to us, we can only see

about 4.6 percent of it, the rest being invisible 'dark matter' and 'dark energy' but we have absolutely no idea what those things are.

7. The entropy of a sphere is equivalent to its surface area, not its volume. Entropy can be thought of as increasing disorder in the universe; things progress from order towards chaos. Entropy can be measured and our measurements suggest that the amount of entropy in the universe is equivalent to what we would find if it were two dimensional (flat) rather than the three dimensional structure we observe. This is one of the reasons that scientists are currently speculating that the universe may be a hologram. If you want to study these ideas more deeply, you might like to read *The Black Hole War* by Leonard Susskind who, incidentally, has made available hundreds of his Stanford University physics lectures, free of charge, on YouTube.

Is the Universe a Hologram?

A hologram is a three-dimensional image projected from a two-dimensional image by bouncing light off its surface and creating interference patterns.

So the four-dimensional spacetime we call our universe could be created from something three-dimensional and, in theory, four dimensions could give rise to five and so on. Going backwards, since 3D can arise from 2D, perhaps 2D can arise from 1D.

If we take 3D to refer to anything that has height, length and width and 2D as something that is flat like a sheet of paper or the surface of a table, having only length and width but no height, and 1D as a straight line which has only length but no height or width, we can get some idea of what we mean by these dimensions and we will return to this shortly.

But first, let's have a look at a suggestion, which has been made recently, that if the universe is indeed a hologram, it must be projected from a 2D surface such as the inside surface of a sphere. Imagine a huge sphere within which the whole universe is suspended. This theory would possibly explain our strange discovery about the entropy of the universe, as discussed above.

In my opinion, this idea seems a bit back to front. If there is a sphere generating our infinitely big, expanding universe then the sphere is also infinitely expanding and moving away from what it is projecting. If it has an inner surface, it must also have an outer one and a sphere is itself a three-dimensional shape, so what projected that? And what lies outside it?

It seems more reasonable to suppose that, rather than being projected from the outside in, the universe would be more likely to be projected from the inside out. A very small sphere also has a 2D outside surface that could give rise to a 3D image that is infinitely large and perhaps something one-dimensional within that small sphere could, in theory, give rise to it.

We would have to be very careful here in defining what exactly we mean by one dimensional.

If you look at a stretched out piece of string from the other side of a room, it might look like a straight line but as you approach you see that the string has a thickness to it that makes it look more like a long, very thin rectangle. As you get nearer still you see that it also has depth and is actually a very long, thin cylindrical object and is therefore three-dimensional. For it to be one dimensional, it would have to be so narrow that it would remain one-dimensional at whatever magnification.

Now in physics there is a distance which cannot be further reducible. It's called the Plank length. So we can now propose the existence of a piece of "string" one plank length in diameter. Its length could be infinite or it could be only one Plank length long. It could exist as a free "string" or its ends could be joined together to form a loop. Were it to be used to generate a 2D object, it could give rise to a flat membrane, one Plank length thick (in order for this to be truly two dimensional) or fold around to form a tube, a tiny sphere, a bubble or other three-dimensional shape with a 2D surface.

So we arrive by an unusual route at string theory and our ideas of reality begin to converge with those of others coming at it from different directions.

Let's go further still. If the string was only one Plank length long it would be a single point, a dot one Plank length in diameter. Consulting the works of mathematicians, I have read that a single point can be referred to as zero-dimensional, while 'one-dimensional' refers to a line. Interestingly, I have also read that a hypothetical object one plank length in diameter is likely to be a tiny and very hot black hole, just like the ones proposed by loop quantum gravity theorists. So maybe the universe is constantly being generated from tiny black holes, everywhere, throughout spacetime.

We can reasonably ask ourselves where such tiny black holes, or Zero D objects, came from in the first place. Continuing with our n arising from n-1 law, perhaps we can infer the presence of 'something', Zero minus one maybe, from which our Zero D dot was projected: something which has no dimensions, which in a three dimensional universe means it does not exist. But supposing it does exist, it just has no dimensions, so it would be in the universe but not of the universe and therefore could be both everywhere and nowhere yet not be bound by the physical laws obeyed by the contents of the universe - a bit like the universe itself really.

More food for thought there perhaps?

His disciples said to him, "When will the kingdom come?" "It
will not come by waiting for it. It will not be a matter of
saying 'Here it is' or 'There it is'. Rather the kingdom of the
Father is spreading out upon the earth and men do not see it."

The Gospel of Thomas, Verse 113

News from the I.T. Department

From the field of Information Technology and current research into quantum computing, we find that the more we learn about how to build a quantum computer, the more we discover that the universe itself appears to work that way.

So let's look at what we know about computing:

Computers are designed to store and process information. A bit of information is a digit whose value can be 0 or 1. A qubit is a quantum system which can exist in any or all combinations of 0 and 1 simultaneously. The mysterious spin of an electron, apparently, fits the bill very nicely.

A proton has 40 bits of information and a hydrogen atom, which has just one proton and one electron, has the capacity to encode 4 million bits of information, far beyond anything we have been able to achieve using mere silicon chips; hence the current interest in the development of quantum computers! The human brain has the capacity to encode 10 to the power 44 (1 with 44 zeros after it) bits of information.

There are currently about 7 billion people alive on our planet. Considering the information storage and processing capacity of just one human brain, there arises the possibility that 7 billion human brains have the capacity to generate the known universe as we see it. We don't see all of it at once: the outer bits become more vague and woolly, as do the smallest bits when we try to look at them. We see detail in things that are close up and in areas we are currently looking at and then we make general inferences about the rest, which requires very little processing activity.

Vlatko Vedral, a leading expert in the field of quantum computing, in his excellent book, *Decoding Reality*, has suggested that we might live within a simulation which is constantly "generating us and everything we see around us". Moreover, he asks: "Could it be that there is no other information in the universe than that generated by us as we create our own reality?"

Perhaps, as the great mathematician John Wheeler said: "Physics gives rise to observer participancy: observer participancy gives rise to information; information gives rise to physics."

The guys in the IT department are not the only people to give voice to such thoughts:

> *"Nothing else but your own mind creates your world.*
> *Your world is the product of yourself."*

> *Buddha Maitreya, 13.7.09*

And so we enter the land of the philosophers.

News from the Philosophy Department

Philosophy is a whole discipline that concerns itself with getting to the truth of things. It is so wide-ranging that it includes pretty much all aspects of our existence. You can, if you wish, study the philosophy of economics, logic, ethics, education, politics or what used to be called 'natural philosophy', which is better known these days as 'science', to name but a few.

What we are going to look at here, however, is a particular branch of philosophy called 'metaphysics', which attempts to ask the biggest and most difficult questions, such as:

What is a human being?

What am I?

What is happiness?

What is mind?

What is consciousness?

What is wisdom?

What is important in life?

…and so on.

In other words, it looks at all the kinds of questions we are asking ourselves in our present quest for enlightenment.

This is not simply an academic exercise that we engage in just to satisfy our curiosity; there is also the underlying hope that, from what we infer about reality, we might develop insights that allow us to live more ethically and find meaning and purpose in our lives.

While we don't want to turn our study of philosophy into a study of philosophers and philosophical categories (as many textbooks tend to do), let's have a look at what could be useful to us right now among the many philosophical ideas that have emerged over millennia. Each of these various ideas gives rise to a particular school of thought that is usually labelled with a word ending in "…ism". A person who decides that a particular idea is the most likely to be valid is therefore labelled an "…ist", though it is possible, and perhaps desirable, for any philosopher to weigh up the pros and cons of any argument and keep an open mind about 'ultimate truth', if such a thing exists.

Some philosophical viewpoints

Think carefully about each of the following viewpoints in turn.

View 1 - Dualism.

Mind and body are separate things and the mind does not depend on the body in order to exist; it can exist on its own as a 'soul'.

This is known as *Cartesian Dualism* (or substance dualism). Essentially it is the view that you are not your body, you are a kind of invisible and insubstantial presence that is just occupying your body on a temporary basis until it is no longer required, after which you kind of slip out of it and leave it behind like an old set of clothes. Plato was one of the people who believed in this separation of the soul from the body when we die. The most popular world religions are founded on this belief, one offshoot of which is that a separate soul may be rewarded or punished after death for its behaviour while in this body.

"You don't have a soul. You are a soul. You have a body."

C.S. Lewis

The widespread popularity of this view could suggest that it is the most likely explanation, based on our own experience of reality. Then again, it could also imply that a majority of people don't like the idea of their body coming to an end but find it comforting to think that, if they are good, they will enjoy eternal pleasure after the body dies. An even stronger motive may be that they don't want to take the risk of eternal suffering if they behave badly or don't buy into this idea.

Ironically, another type of dualism is that God is somehow separate from ourselves: perhaps the most limiting idea ever to have arisen out of religion. It is possible to sing the hymn: "God be in my head and in my understanding; God be in my eyes and in my looking; God be in my mouth and in my speaking; God be in my heart and in my thinking" while still imagining God as kind of hitching a lift for a moment or two before going off to some destination 'out there' until we kneel down to pray and invite Him in again. Could it be that God is always looking out through our eyes and that the only reason we find it so hard to find God is that what we are looking for is that which is doing the looking?

View 2 - Materialism.

Only the body exists. Mind, or consciousness, is just an epiphenomenon generated by the brain.

This is a commonly-held position among scientists. It suggests that only physical objects exist, there is no such thing as a 'soul' and the whole universe arose as some kind of cosmic accident which, although it has evolved and given rise to us, has no inherent meaning. Taken to the extreme, this view may lead to a thing called nihilism, which is possibly the gloomiest of all philosophical standpoints, as it suggests that everything, even life itself, is pointless.

Not all scientists are nihilists, however. Everything we have learned so far from our scientific investigations of reality, from the subatomic to the universal, including the workings of the cells inside our own body, is already sufficient to fill us with unending awe! Albert Einstein saw that materialistic science was not incompatible with spirituality and suggested what he described as a "cosmic religious sense" which does not involve any kind of dogma or the idea of a God made in man's own image but appreciates the "nobility and marvellous order which are revealed in nature and in the world of thought" and in which a person "seeks to experience the totality of existence as a unity full of significance." He found it ironic that people who were inspired by their highest religious experience were variously judged to be heretics, atheists or saints.

View 3 - Solipsism.

Only my mind exists. In other words, bodies - whether we are talking here about my body or anyone else's - are just illusions created by my mind.

This view is the opposite of materialism and is a kind of super-trip of the ego. It is understandable, in that I have no real way of knowing anything about how you see the world. I could assume that you experience the colour red the same way I do but, even if neither of us happens to be colour blind, there is no way that I can be sure that I am correct in that assumption. As a guy called Wittgenstein said, "If all words get their meaning from my experience, then what I mean by 'experience' is 'my experience'". Potential problems with solipsism are a) that you might not consider other people to be particularly important if you don't believe that they exist - with potential consequences for the way you treat them - and b) that if you go around saying that you, and only you, are God and everyone else is just a product of your own imagination, you might get yourself locked away. But be careful before you dismiss it out of hand. Our dreams seem very real to us until we wake up, so you never know, this whole show that we are calling 'reality' could all be 'but a dream' or what is known in the East as the illusion of maya. Incidentally, maya does not necessarily imply that the universe does not exist, only that we are looking at it wrongly and have not yet glimpsed the hidden fabric underlying it. A lot depends on who or what it is that you think you are!

View 4 - Monism.

There is only one mind, or consciousness, which views itself though separate identities created out of itself. What prevents us from seeing this underlying unity is the ego (our idea of being an individual, separate self).

Monism is the idea that only one kind of substance exists, so materialism can also be classed as a type of monism. For materialists, only physical substance exists, an assumption that rests, perhaps, on slightly shakier ground since the discovery that matter and energy are interchangeable and seventy percent of the universe appears to be composed of 'dark energy' - and we don't yet know what that is.

Another type of monism is idealism. For idealists, only mind exists, so whatever exists is either a mind or is dependent on a mind for its existence, therefore the above definition could be classed as idealistic monism. This idea lies at the heart of many Eastern Philosophies and religions and could be said to underlie many others if we go back far enough, beyond the trappings and misinterpretations and the dualistic idea that 'God' is somehow separate from us.

When we look to the heart of the original teachings of most religions, we find a common thread that has been proclaimed by the great sages, yet is difficult for most thinkers in the West to understand and accept. Having said that, it has become more widely accepted in the West in recent decades and has been espoused by eminent scientists such as Erwin Schrödinger: "The overall number of minds is just one" and Max Plank: "This mind is the matrix of all matter." These views came, not from their religious ideologies but from their scientific observations of how matter, or energy, behaves in the quantum realm.

That's a lot to take in!

So now, it might be useful for you to pause and have a think about each of the above viewpoints. Do any of them strike a chord with you? Do any of them bring about an emotional response, either for or against?

Sometimes, we may have a powerful negative reaction to something that sounds very wrong to us and that gives us a clue as to what we do believe, even if we were previously unaware of it. There is also a possibility that we can then put our strong feelings either way to one side, consider all the possibilities and come at the whole subject with fresh eyes that may allow us to glimpse a third perspective that we had not previously considered.

It may even be that there is an overarching view that puts all the presented viewpoints into a wider context without making any of them right or wrong. They may not all be mutually exclusive, just different ways of looking at the same thing, like the people in the following story.

A creature walks into a village where all the inhabitants are blind. Each person approaches the creature and places a hand on it. One says it is like a rope with a small brush attached, one that it is like the sail of a boat, another that it is like a stone trumpet, another that it is like a rough hosepipe, another that it is like a wide pillar. Of course, the creature is an elephant.

Just because two people cannot agree, it does not automatically follow that one of them must be wrong, they may just be looking at the problem from a different, yet equally valid, angle. Even if they are looking at exactly the same thing, they may interpret what they see in different ways. This brings us naturally to the point where we need to ask questions about how our minds work, so it's time to take a look at a few of the useful insights we have gained from the study of psychology.

News from the Psychology Department

Clearly, it is not an easy task to discover which of our experiences are 'authentic' and which are a kind of delusion generated by our own minds. Transcendental experiences aside, can we even believe what we see with our own eyes? From the field of psychology, we learn that we only see about ten percent of what is in front of us. The other ninety percent is generated by our brains from our expectations. This is why magicians' tricks can so easily deceive us. Experiments have shown that if we watch a magician juggling balls, we will continue to see the balls being thrown upwards even after the magician secretly palmed one of them and didn't throw it up. Our brain saw what it expected to see, even though it wasn't there.

Our eyes are only partly responsible for our ability to see. Incoming patterns of light give rise to signals in the brain from which a partial image is created; the rest of the details are filled in by our own minds.

This is not normally a problem for us, as the approximation of reality that our brain cooks up for us is usually more than adequate for our day to day survival, unless we happen to be providing a witness testimony in court and can't agree on the colour of a car or we allow our recollection of events to be distorted by leading questions.

In our quest to find out what is actually true, it is also worth remembering that we only see a narrow bunch of wavelengths in the middle of a wide electromagnetic spectrum that includes gamma rays, X-rays, radio waves, ultra-violet, infra-red and various other stuff that we can't see without special equipment. Even with that equipment, we only get to see about four percent of what is actually there. On top of that, there is 'dark matter' and the even more mysterious 'dark energy' that is believed to constitute seventy percent of our universe. As we read these words, billions of invisible neutrinos are passing through our own bodies every second but detecting even one of them requires a monumental feat of scientific and technical genius. Our perception of reality then, even when we are fully sober, wide awake and well informed, is woefully limited.

If we can't rely wholly on our own senses, especially our eyes, what then are we to make of any more unusual perceptions we may experience?

The God Spot

Neuroscientists tell us that there is a region of the brain – two actually: one on each side of the head – that they have called 'the God Spot'.

This impressive title comes from the observation that when you stick electrodes into this particular point in a living, conscious brain, the owner of that brain has 'transcendental' experiences similar to those reported by experienced meditators.

Now we could see this as evidence that any kind of transcendental experience is just an illusion generated from stimulation of the God Spot, perhaps by small seizures, hysteria, wishful thinking, not eating properly or some other means, but perhaps we might be looking at things from back to front.

Let's suppose, just for the sake of this argument, that each of us is like a kind of biological computer that has hardware (our body and it's brain) on which a software programme is running (our ego) which sees itself as a separate, autonomous entity. Unbeknown to each machine, all of these various computers (me, you and everyone else) are connected to the internet (a kind of super-awesome pan-galactic entity that is aware of the whole thing) .

Now suppose an isolated computer had a wireless modem and, while it was disconnected from the internet, you could stimulate that modem to make it think that it was connected to the World Wide Web. Just because you could do that, does it follow that the internet does not actually exist and is just a product of that computer's deranged imagination and wishful thinking? Or does all of this suggest that perhaps the God Spot, if such a thing exists, could be the part of our brain which interfaces with the 'universal internet' and allows those who know how to use it to tune in and experience 'cosmic consciousness'? What do you think?

Weird experiences

Interestingly, as I write this, an article has just been published in *New Scientist* magazine describing a study in which volunteers taking the Mexican hallucinogenic drug ayahuasca reported exactly the same kind of effects as other people describing 'near-death experiences'. The effects included a feeling of "incredible peace" and "a feeling of unity with the universe".

What is most remarkable about this article is that the findings were taken as evidence that such experiences could be explained by how the brain works and were 'not evidence of paranormal phenomena'. Now that depends on what we mean by 'paranormal' – a word with so many negative connotations that it relegates the whole notion to the realms of unscientific nonsense dreamed up by people with no scientific training who will believe in everything from haunted houses to telepathy with aliens.

This, in my opinion, is incredibly irresponsible, for all the reasons discussed above in our consideration of the 'God Spot'. The given interpretation may again be back to front. What if it is possible for the human brain to become enlightened: to see our unity with everything? What if certain chemicals facilitate this process?

Personally, I have resisted any temptation to experiment with mind-altering substances during my lifetime because I decided at the age of about ten that, if I had any kind of mystical experience, I wanted to make sure that it was authentic and not some kind of drug-induced hallucination. Therefore, I am in no way suggesting that we should all partake of illegal substances. Quite apart from not wishing to encourage you to get on the wrong side of the law, or risk taking a nose-dive down the particularly slippery social slope that addiction has on offer, I seriously don't consider it a good idea to mess with your head in that way if you truly want to understand reality and possibly help to save the world.

However, I am open to the possibility that there could be a substance that facilitates the natural process of awakening and that this particular chemical, if used safely in a clinical setting, might help people to wake up to their connectedness at a time when that awakening is perhaps our best chance of survival into the next century. Even if this did not turn out to be the case, then it is surely worth exploring whether or not this substance might help people with mental health problems, such as chronic depression or obsessive compulsive disorder, for example, to take a wider view of reality that allows them to overcome the feelings of separateness and isolation that can make their lives so difficult. Recent research, such as that reported by Robin Carhart-Harris and Stephen Ross, has suggested that the controlled use of the mushroom-derived chemical psilocybin may be helpful in this respect.

Even weirder experiences

Whatever you think about tales of out-of-body experiences, lots of people appear to have them. At a conference organised by *New Scientist* magazine, which I attended recently, about a fifth of the audience claimed to have had one, and the visiting speaker said that this was typical of the audiences she had put this question to elsewhere. These were all either scientists or people with a strong interest in science who might not be expected to be given to flights of fancy and self-delusion.

Since I can't speak for all of them, I will stick to a couple of examples from closer to home: strange events experienced by members of my own family.

One of these occurred on the waters of lake Coniston when my husband's canoe overturned. As he struggled to free himself from the boat, he watched himself from far away under the water, then from above, and finally witnessed his body pop up at the side of the canoe, gasping for air, at which point he returned to it.

Even stranger is an out-of-body experience that seems to defy not only space but time as well. I was driving down a road one afternoon, having picked up my very young daughter from school. As I rounded a corner, I noticed a car ready to pull out from a side road. I had the right of way and continued on but then the car suddenly took off and pulled out in front of me. Fortunately, I was not going very fast and managed to stop level with the side street but the front corner of my car touched the back corner of the other car as I came to a halt. The other driver apologised and admitted responsibility and we exchanged details. While we were doing this, a lady walked up to us and said that she had witnessed the whole thing but then she walked off again before I had a chance to ask her name and number.

So far, so unremarkable. Then the strange thing happened. When I got back into my car, my daughter was crying. I asked her what was wrong. The impact had been so slight that she could not have been injured. She explained that she was crying because she had seen the whole thing before it happened. Not only that, but she had seen it through a window on the other side of the road, before we even came around the corner. I looked to where she was pointing and had an idea. After comforting my daughter, I went up to the house with the window she claimed to have seen it through and knocked on the door. Sure enough, the person who came to the door was the lady who had witnessed the incident.

The only way I can begin to fathom what might have happened that afternoon is as some kind of non-local quantum field effect. Perhaps the minds of the witness and my daughter were overlapping in some kind of superposition for that brief moment. We may never know, but a combination of the above events has convinced me that there is a lot more to reality that we are currently aware of.

Changes in perception – disorder or ability?

There is a rather unhelpful tendency, especially in the West, for the medical profession to label anything out of the ordinary as a 'syndrome' a 'disorder' or a 'condition' rather than as an ability.

A prime example of this is a phenomenon known as Alice in Wonderland Syndrome or Todd's syndrome, since it was described by a Doctor John Todd in the 1950s. Intentionally or not, this seemingly derogatory term makes it sound as though the person experiencing it is indulging in some kind of fantasy, especially as it is particularly common in children.

Although it is described on some websites as a 'rare condition', it is estimated that it affects ten to twenty percent of the population at some time in their lives, according to Heidi Moawab M.D. in the Neurology Times, in 2016. The incidence may be higher than this because it normally lasts for only a few seconds or minutes and so most people may not consider it worth consulting a doctor about. In fact, neurologists report having heard of it many times in casual conversations with people who, until they brought up the subject, had not thought it worth mentioning to anyone.

The experience has been documented widely and the Neurology Times calls it 'one of the most fascinating neurological symptoms described in the medical literature'.

So let's have a look at what it is. I was particularly fascinated to hear about this phenomenon because I have experienced it myself, particularly as a child.

I recall it as a strange feeling of being very big or very small, usually as I lay in bed ready to drift off to sleep. My legs felt as enormous as tree trunks and there was a 'thickness' around me, invisible like the air but infinitely huge and palpable. It was frightening only because it was so strange and I didn't know what it was. Usually it would disappear as soon as I moved at all or opened my eyes, though sometimes it could last for several minutes or even half an hour. On the occasions where I managed to get out of bed and stagger along to my parents' bedroom, along a floor that seemed endless and to be disappearing under my feet, my mum felt that she had to try to drag me back to reality from wherever it was that I had gone. I recall one occasion in my teens when, while recovering from the flu, I went all the way downstairs from my attic bedroom to the living room where my mother and aunt were having a conversation. I was standing close to the fireplace where I noticed that the walls were insubstantial and not really there and my mum and aunt seemed very far away.

For decades, I could find no one who knew what I was talking about, and I was frustrated by my own inability to put it into words. Every time it happened I would try to hold onto it long enough to allow me to find a way to describe it but the harder I tried to define it, the faster it slipped away. The best way to keep it there was to simply lay perfectly still and watch it without trying to describe it or hold onto it. As a child. I assumed that it was indeed a thing my mum called 'DTs' until years later when I heard about *delirium tremens*, which is something entirely different.

Later, as I scientist, I was both perplexed and intrigued and my best hypothesis was that it was a kind of half-way stage between waking and sleep, like stepping onto the holodeck of the Starship Enterprise when the illusion of infinite space had been generated but the details of the holographic scenery was yet to be added. Perhaps it was the REM state of the mind kicking in but not yet latched onto any kind of visual imagery that would create a dreamscape. That idea seemed very unsatisfactory, however, as this weird distortion of perception was very different from the usual experience of drifting off to sleep and it could continue as I walked around the house. Somnambulism perhaps? But I was not prone to sleepwalking and I wasn't actually dreaming. On the occasion when I had the flu, I could still see my mum and my aunt and listen to what they were saying and engage in normal conversation with them, even while the weird feeling persisted and the walls remained insubstantial.

Another hypothesis might be that there was a blurring of the boundaries between the REM state and the waking state, as may be the case when people suffering from schizophrenia experience hallucinations. These transient experiences, especially the longer one when I had the flu, could be a glimpse of how people experience the world when extreme stress, lack of sleep or other causes distort their vision of the world for longer periods of time. This theory was also unconvincing since I have never been prone to hallucinations or any kind of mental health problems and I was not unusually stressed or tired and I was actually making a good recovery from the flu and feeling much better.

It is only recently that a young person described her experience to me and told me that she had found a community of other people on the internet who told her that it was 'Alice in Wonderland Syndrome'.

Here is her description of her own experiences:

"It only happens very occasionally, when you are not really expecting it. You'll be drifting off to sleep and suddenly you'll start to lose your sense of perception for imagined objects. You'll experience feelings, sensations and images that are familiar to you yet you cannot remember them fully or recreate them again outside of when it's happening naturally. It's like your ability to perceive shape and size has shut down before the rest of your sleeping brain, and suddenly

everything you imagine is simultaneously infinitely large and infinitely small: even the size of yourself, your bed and your bedroom. You are, at the same time, as big as the universe and as small as the tiniest atom. You truly, finally understand the concept of infinity, because your size is infinite in both directions."

That pretty much sums up what I had spent decades trying, without success, to put into words.

Clearly, this is an odd experience that may have many different explanations and more research is obviously needed. However, it is not something that you could ask volunteers to do at will, inside an MRI scanner or an EEG device, since most people agree that it is impossible to bring it on at will.

An association with illness appears to be quite common and, for about six percent of those who are known to have experienced it, it seems to be associated with migraine headaches. However, at least fifty percent of the people who have reported these strange experiences were perfectly well at the time. Moreover, since people with accompanying problems such as illness or headaches might be more likely to mention it to their doctor, then the link with adverse health symptoms may not be as pronounced as it seems.

Most reported cases involve children, possibly because they actually experience it more often than adults or perhaps because they are likely to tell their parents about it and they, in turn, are worried enough to tell a doctor. From what is known so far, the tendency to have these experiences seems to run in families, but again, this may be because people who have experienced it themselves may be more able to recognise what their child is talking about.

The medical consensus is that the process is not harmful, is not a hallucination and is not a sign of any kind of mental illness or cerebrovascular or neurological disease. In casual conversation with neuroscientists, a much higher percentage of people report such events than would be expected from recorded statistics, since most had never considered it worth mentioning to a doctor until asked for examples of altered perception. Like myself, most people appear to be unaware that it has an actual name and may be quite relieved to know that others have experienced it too. In other words, it appears to be a normal, natural process experienced by a large percentage of the population, and it seems stronger in childhood – a condition we tend to grow out of as we get past our teens.

In my own case, the fear I felt was because of the unfamiliarity and the inability of adults to understand or explain to me what was happening. Grown-ups are supposed to know everything, right? In later years it was no longer scary but merely inspired curiosity.

Looking at it now, I can see that there are a variety of explanations and no doubt neuroscientists will pursue the more biological and psychological of these. There is even the suggestion that cough medicine or flu remedies might be to blame, and that may indeed be the case, though it doesn't explain the majority of times when it occurs while people are perfectly well and not taking medication.

What I would like to consider here is the possibility that, rather than a medicalised 'condition', this may be better described as an ability of human beings to experience, not a distorted sense of reality but a fuller awareness of reality. If this sounds far-fetched, look at what we have just discussed about the insights gained through scientific study of the universe. Space and time are not what we think they are. People with AWS frequently report changes in their perception of time as well as space. Is it not possible that they are glimpsing a more accurate picture of reality?

I am not suggesting that these experiences were a type of 'enlightenment'. They were fleeting and in no way the same as the lasting realisation of unity that transformed my own life in 1993. They were strange incidents, certainly, but were not transformative in any way. As a child, I found them to be more worrying than enlightening and they did not involve any kind of peace, bliss or other stuff reported by sages. However, I feel they do deserve further investigation by both scientists and philosophers, as they suggest that our ability as a species to experience deeper levels of reality is still evolving and there is the possibility that we have untapped potential that could be very useful in our efforts to wake ourselves up in time to save our world.

In order to glimpse such potential, we will need to gain a better understanding of what we mean by the word 'consciousness'.

The Science of 'Consciousness'

> *"I regard consciousness as fundamental. I regard matter as derivative from consciousness. We cannot get behind consciousness. Everything that we talk about, everything that we regard as existing, postulates consciousness."*

> *Max Planck*

We may have explored every inch of our world, studied the surface of neighbouring planets, mapped billions of galaxies and traced the existence of our universe back to the Big Bang but discovering how we happen to be conscious of such things remains perhaps the greatest challenge to our collective imagination and ingenuity.

Until very recently, however, any scientist voicing an interest in researching the nature of consciousness risked saying a simultaneous "goodbye" to both their funding and their credibility. Fortunately, that situation has now changed, with 'consciousness' making a fairly dramatic transition from pseudoscience to buzz-word in recent years

When *New Scientist* magazine held two conferences on the subject in London, I found the huge auditorium packed with eager listeners on both occasions. Such events have become a regular feature in the US, with annual events taking place in Arizona and elsewhere.

When I attended the London conference in 2016, I came away quite disappointed, having discovered that this subject was still in its infancy, though careful gropings had yielded a few interesting, if tentative, findings. Lectures by top researchers in the field described the progress of diverse lines of enquiry, from Artificial Intelligence to what is happening inside the brains of people in a comatose or 'vegetative' state and whether or not animals can be considered to be conscious. Subsequent progress in these areas has allowed people with 'locked in syndrome' to communicate with the outside world and has led to a consensus that many animals are conscious, intelligent creatures who are able to experience pain and emotions just as we do and are capable of letting us know whether they choose one thing or another or remain undecided. This latter ability is not confined to dolphins or other mammals but is even found in birds.

Perhaps the most promising titbit offered during that first conference was that 'qualia' – the hard-to-explain stuff like our ability to perceive colour and appreciate music – may be four-dimensional states arising from our three-dimensional brain structures. More recent research has suggested that consciousness may arise a result of transient seven-dimensional states arising and collapsing in the brain, as reported in *New Scientist* in September 2017.

The follow-up conference in 2018 found scientists becoming somewhat more daring, with some admitting to having had out of body experiences and informing us that the world is watching us at the same time that we are watching it.

A common theme was that we don't just passively perceive our world, we consciously create it. Our brains appear to be engaged in an ongoing process of prediction and error-minimising, comparing input signals received via the senses with what we expected, and perception is a minimisation of prediction errors. When lots of us agree on our perceptions, we call that 'reality', but it's still the brain's best guess of the causes of the sensory inputs it receives, by comparing them with our expectations, beliefs and prior experience.

As an example, they played us a recording of a weird and incomprehensible noise and then we were given a sentence in English. When they played the sound again, we were able to hear, quite clearly, those words within it – the conclusion being that we can only hear words if we have already heard them. This is consistent with accounts of the native inhabitants of North America being unable to see the ships of the first European explorers until they landed on the beach.

The research so far appears to be telling us that we try to reduce errors by creating better predictions. Such findings underline the power of our expectations in shaping our perception of reality and suggest that our predictions become self-fulfilling prophecies, which is something we will return to again in later chapters.

Neuroscience has indeed made considerable advances over the past couple of decades, with various types of scanners being able to chart the firing and wiring of the cells that make up our brains. There may come a time when such machines will be able to read our thoughts.

As interesting as all of this may be, however, we are still very much attached to explanations of consciousness as physical, biological processes. Oddly, none of the speakers at either of the *New Scientist* conferences I attended mentioned the possible involvement of non-local quantum field effects in the brain, though this is a line of inquiry that is currently being pursued by others. Since quantum field effects appear to be involved in biological processes such as photosynthesis - the way that plants use sunlight as an energy source for building sugars from carbon dioxide and water - and in the navigational abilities of migrating birds, it is not such a leap of faith to suppose that they may also be involved in how our own brains work. Some tentative work with fruit flies resistant to anaesthetics, by Luca Turin and his team, suggests that consciousness may be related to the direction of spin of electrons in the brain, though this remains controversial. Although general anaesthetics are widely used and very successful in rendering people unconscious, we don't yet really understand how they work at all or even whether or not 'consciousness' is the correct word to use for whatever it is that we are attempting to describe.

During an intriguing conversation with a professor of anaesthesiology and a professor of neurology and neuroscience, at Harvard Medical School, an Indian mystic, Sadhguru, suggested that the word they should be using was 'wakefulness' and that our experience of being awake and of time passing is variable and is dependent on memory. When we first wake up in the morning, some of us are very alert while others are pretty much out of it until after their first cup of coffee. When we wake, even from a deep and dreamless sleep, we have the impression that time has passed.

When we are anaesthetised, however, a common experience is that time seems to have vanished. What the anaesthesiologists described, I can verify by my own experience. I remember laying on a trolley, waiting to go into the theatre for an operation, and being told by a medical attendant that I had already been in there for over an hour. I

94

thought he was joking! He wasn't. Somehow, between my framing a particular question in my mind and saying it aloud, an hour or more had gone by without my noticing. This was not simply the inability to recall an event that I knew had taken place, it was as if a bit of my timeline had been cut out and the ends seamlessly stitched together, like some weird magician's trick, resulting in a feeling of disbelief that anything had happened at all.

It appears that the field of anaesthesiology might prove a rich ground for further study into the differences between the levels of consciousness or wakefulness and perhaps such studies will shed some light on what consciousness actually is.

A nice little factoid I picked up at the second *New Scientist* Consciousness conference in London was that the brain has 100,000 neurons that can exist in more states than there are atoms in the known universe. Cool. Let these jiggle themselves into seven-dimensional configurations, add quantum non-locality across spacetime within a holographic pattern of vibrating energy that is a participatory simulation generated by our own minds and we have a whole load of exciting possibilities to explore!

The more we learn about the universe through our observations, experiments and logical reasoning, the more we are taken towards conclusions that we did not anticipate: time, space and matter do not exist in the way we think they do; something very weird is going on. When we look for the building blocks of matter, instead of hard particles, we find energy fields and vibrations and we see that mass and energy are interchangeable and what we perceive to be particles are ephemeral things that are constantly coming and going. Instead of universal, constant time, we find that time is relative and dependent on the velocities of objects travelling through space. What we observe to be real is no more than a mental construct of information received via our limited senses, which tells us very little about what's actually 'out there', if anything. And when it comes to understanding what it is that is aware of all the above phenomena, we honestly haven't a clue.

Observation, enquiry and reasoning can only help us to a point. We reach the limit of their usefulness when we realise that anything we observe implies that there is an object to be observed and an observer to do the observing. Whenever we try to see what the observer is, we make it into the object we are observing. However, it is still useful to ask this question: "What am I?".

> *"It is like the universe screams in your face: "Do you know what I am? How Grand I am? Can you even comprehend what I am? What are you compared to me?" And when you know enough science, you can just smile up at the universe and reply, "Dude, I am you!""*
>
> *Phil Hellenes, in his inspiring YouTube video "Science Saved My Soul".*

Chapter 2 - What Religions Can Tell Us

Before we even get started on this one, I need to say that I am not about to ask you to give up your religion, if you have one, or to get one if you don't. I won't be inviting you to become an atheist or an agnostic, or advocating the virtues of one religion over another, or being judgemental or over-critical about the beliefs you currently hold.

After decades of studying various religions, as well as all the sciences, I have come to the conclusion that science and religion are not diametrically opposed but are simply different ways of looking at how things are and trying to make sense of it all. The scientist David Bohm invited us to imagine a glass aquarium with people standing around it looking at the same fish. Some could only see the head, others only the tail and others one side or the other. None of them were wrong: they were just seeing the same fish from different angles. Perhaps it's the same with reality.

If we are to survive as a species, I feel that there is more to be gained from a sharing of ideas than competing to see who is right.

Are We Actually Singing from the Same Hymn Sheet?

"I believe in God, but not as one thing, not as an old man in the sky. I believe that what people call God is something in all of us. I believe that what Jesus and Mohammed and Buddha and all the rest said was right. It's just that the translations have gone wrong."

John Lennon

If we look very closely at the world's religions, we may discover strands of wisdom that appear to underlie most, if not all of them. Aldous Huxley referred to this as the "Perennial Philosophy".

A religious leader I spoke to a few years ago described this approach as "shopping around" or "pick 'n' mix" and was quite upset by the idea. To me, it was the equivalent of being shocked that someone who bought their bananas from Tesco might buy bread from their local corner shop and salad from Sainsbury's and, in the process, see that they were all, in essence, purveyors of groceries.

Another suggested that I was actually "window shopping" and couldn't reap the full benefit of a religion unless I went inside and immersed myself in it completely. Well actually, done that but, nice as these places are, I wouldn't like to spend my life inside a supermarket.

My personal opinion is that there is much to be gained from looking at what religion might offer us in our attempt to understand ourselves, our world and our place within it if there is any possibility that such insights can help to unite us as a species and improve our chances of survival into the next century.

"Like the bee gathering honey from different flowers, the wise person accepts the essence of the different scriptures and sees only the good in all religions."

Ghandi

Whether or not you subscribe to any religion, you may still benefit greatly from having a closer look at all of them. By that, I don't mean examining all the roots, stories, rites and rituals. We're not looking at differences here, we're looking at what it is that unites us: what it is that could bring us all peace and make us free.

We are asking this at a time when the power of the world's religions to influence us appears to be declining. Whether we consider that to be a heartening or worrying trend, let's have a look at how things are and what we can learn from it all.

Is Religion a Thing of the Past?

Recent WIN-Gallup polls, such as the one in 2016 that recorded the beliefs of 66,000 men and women across 68 countries, found that the number of people claiming to be religious has fallen significantly over the last couple of decades. While around sixty percent of the world's population still identified themselves as 'religious' only thirteen percent described themselves as 'atheists'. Of the rest, many said that they simply didn't care either way.

However, studies have shown that, even in secular societies, a majority of people still claim to believe in some kind of 'higher power' or 'spiritual being', whether or not they engage in religious practices such as prayer or attendance at a place of worship, and even committed atheists may be unopposed to 'unscientific' ideas such as astrology or the law of Karma and may still believe in the existence of an immortal soul.

Human beings appear to be hard-wired to share an intuition that there is more to reality than we are able to prove or to measure, and this persists in our modern world despite the rise of science and technology. Why, we may ask, do we do this? What evolutionary advantages might we have gained from looking at the world in this way?

Are Religions Harmful or Helpful?

While I don't subscribe to any particular religion, I am not dismissive of their value either. Social scientists, psychologists and historians have argued that religion has played a key role in bringing people together to form communities and civilisations and that this has allowed us not only to survive within our global environment but to dominate it, though I'll leave you to be the judge of whether or not that is a good thing.

Quite apart from the obvious advantage of having some kind of insurance policy for our immortal soul - which may help us to overcome some of the existential anguish relating to our inevitable demise by guaranteeing us eternal rewards in the afterlife if we do our best in this one - perhaps the "threats of hell and hopes of paradise" thing may have modified some of our least helpful tendencies and made us learn to get on with each other. Then again, recent research, such as the global analysis by Zuckerman in 2009, has revealed that secular societies tend to have lower rates of crime, infant mortality, teenage pregnancies and suicide and enjoy more health and wealth and a longer life expectancy.

Of course, there could be a chicken and egg situation here. Perhaps people who already enjoy good health, wealth, safety and job security can afford not to require the reassuring presence of a divine being and are more likely to be tolerant of others. According to Gallup-international.com: "It is evident that all those countries which feel stable and not threatened show low levels of religious, cultural or racial superiority. And vice versa."

Nations appear to become more focussed on religion when they are experiencing serious internal conflicts, instability and periods of rapid change leading to greater insecurity.

So when the going gets tough, and perhaps we feel threatened or fearful that there will not be enough to go around, we may have a tendency to become both more religious and less tolerant of others,

100

while greater security has the opposite effect and our society naturally becomes more secular.

It is possible that, without dependence on a higher power to intervene on our behalf, or the opportunity to get things right in some future incarnation if we mess up in the here and now, we might be more likely to take greater responsibility for our actions in this lifetime, though the underlying psychology may be complex and subtle and many factors may interact to determine our behaviour.

The ethical focus of many religious teachings may have helped some people to be fine and upstanding pillars of their community but research has also shown that we tend to behave better when we believe that we are being watched. The idea of surveillance by a kind of cosmic CCTV that sees our every action, monitors our thoughts and punishes transgressions with eternal damnation might provide us with a fairly powerful motive for good behaviour, providing we all agree on what we mean by 'good behaviour' and don't think we get to score extra points by eliminating anyone who doesn't agree with us.

We do appear to have a tendency to form 'in-groups' and pick fights with people who come across as 'different', and this has led to endless suffering in the name of our various 'faiths'. When combined with political and cultural objectives, this tendency has undoubtedly played a role in the dividing up of our land masses into the various nations and states we have today.

Despite the obviously detrimental effects of conflicts between those nations, or the sub-groups within them, we could also consider the positive benefits to individual nations and communities of sharing a story about how the world was created and how it works, which only becomes harmful if the story is never allowed to become modified in the light of new information.

Perhaps more importantly, societies may be united by social attitudes, which are particularly helpful if they include an ethos of kindness, cooperation, community and tolerance. If that kind of ethos could exist between all nations rather than just within the boundaries of each, this world might perhaps be a more comfortable place to live in. Sadly, as we look around us, we see supposedly peace-loving peoples living next door to each other and prepared to fight to the death to defend their own particular version of the faith they subscribe to and we obsess about minor differences resulting mostly from historical perspectives or interpretations of scriptures.

At this stage in our evolution, surely we have the capacity to rise above these surface differences and develop an ethos that we can all agree upon, not because it was imposed upon us by some particular person or divine being but because, as human beings, these are the shared values that we, all of us, consider to be the hallmark of our humanity. We have tried this before, with our documents supporting human rights. Perhaps it is time to sit down together, yet again, with all nations and all faiths having the opportunity to contribute, and draw up a list of the values that we all agree to live by. Whether we call it a 'global human rights charter' or a 'multi-faith code of conduct' or whatever, perhaps we could agree to live together in peace. A bit like the United Nations but with everybody in on it and totally up for it this time.

You may well look around you at the current state of global affairs and shake your head at the seeming impossibility of bringing about such a 'utopia' in this world. What kind of world-view, you may well ask, could possibly be shared by such a diverse species with all its entrenched and often diametrically-opposed views? Well, that's basically what this book is about, and it isn't something new: it's a world-view that has been proposed by sages and philosophers from every faith and every nation for millennia: the view that we can put aside our differences and live together in peace because, ultimately, we are all one. And yes, even our egocentric and, in some cases, possibly psychopathic world leaders need to buy into this. Election-rigging, intimidation and social media hacking aside, their power still comes from our votes and we can vote for peacekeepers instead of narcissistic warmongers if we choose to.

Whether we have already subscribed to a particular religion or whether we consider ourselves to be scientifically-minded atheists living in a secular society, or whether we are just currently undecided about such matters or don't have any particular interest in the subject at all, we can ask: What can any or all of the world's religions tell us that might help us to become aware of the unity underlying our diversity? In fact, were any of them, perhaps, designed for that purpose in the first place? And do any of the ideas that have been embedded in our religions and cultures for millennia have any relevance today?

Being brought up in a religious household, in a religious neighbourhood where everyone went to church every Sunday wearing their best clothes and a hat, or risked being ostracised as some kind of 'heathen', it seemed to me as a child that everything interesting appeared to have happened two thousand years ago, after which the almighty went off and left us to it. No more miracles. No more voices from the sky or burning bushes or chariots of fire.

But what if it isn't over? What if creation is what is happening right now, all the time, in this moment? And what if we are all actively involved in this creative process? At a subatomic level, that's what our scientific insights appear to be telling us. It's also what the ancients have been shouting at us down the centuries and is still there to be heard if we are ready to listen.

We don't have to use religious terminology if we don't want to, but for those who do, we need to be clear about one thing especially: What do we mean when we talk about God?

If There is Only One God, Which One Are We Talking About?

> "Do not go about worshiping deities and religious institutions as the source of the subtle truth. To do so is to place intermediaries between yourself and the divine, and to make of yourself a beggar who looks outside for a treasure that is hidden inside his own breast."
>
> Lao Tze

Most people following a major religion will say to me that there is only one God. It says so in all of their holy books. Variously described as 'immortal', 'eternal', 'without equal', 'begetting none and begotten by none', the 'One without a second' is 'not two' but simply 'Unity'. Even in India, with its plethora of individual deities, these are all aspects of the one divine Self or Brahman. Yet many people who claim that there can only ever be one God will, in the next breath, speak of their own God as being superior to the God of different religions. Over the centuries, human beings have described their own idea of this one God in various ways: at times jealous, at times demanding, at other times angry enough to do a fair amount of smiting, yet they also appear to agree upon the underlying idea that God is love.

That being so, what need could there be to fight among ourselves? Why not, instead, follow the divine example and love each other?

Most wars, when we look at them closely, appear to be politically motivated. A desire for someone else's land, or a desire for revenge when someone takes our land and kills our family in the process, are perhaps more powerful reasons for going to war than a disagreement over subtle points of philosophy. When religion is brought into the mix, it often seems to be as an afterthought or as an excuse, with out-of-context quotes from scriptures to justify unreasonable or even barbaric behaviour. If God is love, one can only wonder what God would make of the way we treat each other. But is God love? If not, what is God then?

Is it even possible that those of us who believe that God exists – and also those of us who categorically believe that there is no such thing as God in the first place - can all at least agree on what we mean by the word 'God'? What is it that we each profess to disbelieve or to believe in?

What Do We All Mean by God?

"You are looking for God. That is the problem. The God in
you is the one who is looking."

Rumi

In the end, if there is only one God, always everywhere present, all seeing, all knowing and all loving, then it must be the very same God that we all perceive, whatever name or attributes we choose to ascribe to that God. As a scientist, I don't have a problem with the idea of such a God.

If that seems to be a strange thing for a scientist to say, we can ask ourselves a question: If, in the beginning, there was only God and God created everything, what did God create everything out of if not out of God? And if everything was created out of God, how can anything not be God or be separate from God? If everything is God, then God is what we all are: basically the entire Cosmos and everything that supports or sustains it and whatever it may or may not have arisen from and may or may not return to. God is just one name for it. We could just as easily call it the universe, the multiverse or just everything that exists. To say that we are not a part of everything that exists would be nonsense.

How are we to separate ourselves from the universe when we are made from the elements of a planet formed from the dust and gas of exploded stars, and the atoms of our bodies are continuous with those of our biosphere? Moreover, if God is omniscient, omnipresent and so forth, how can God be separate from all of that? How can God not already BE all of that?

If God is all of that and we are part of that, and there is nowhere that God is not then, by definition, we are all part of God rather than God being like an important visitor whom we invite in occasionally to take up residence inside us. How could such a God ever abandon us if God is what we are and always were, from the very beginning?

Science has already revealed to us that time, space and matter are not what we think they are. The more we look, the more we see that the ultimate nature of reality may be a field of fields and that everything arises as vibrations within this underlying fabric of reality. It doesn't matter whether you call it 'underlying fabric' or 'universal field' or 'cosmic quantum ground state' or 'God' or whatever. It's what we are all made of, so we might as well accustom ourselves to the idea that we are made out of this finer 'universal something', whatever we might choose to call it.

"He who knows this is called the knower of the field. Know that I am the knower in all the fields of my creation; and that the wisdom which sees the field and the knower of the field is true wisdom."

The Bhagavad Gita, Chapter 13

The question then becomes: "Fair enough, we are all made out of the same stuff but it's just matter and energy, not a conscious thing, whereas 'God' implies sentience and the universe can't be conscious can it?"

Now I have often heard it said that only the human brain is complex enough to be aware of its own existence. As a biochemist with an interest in neuroscience, I am aware of that complexity and aware of most of the current lines of research into where and how consciousness might arise in the brain. However, when you really look at this argument, perhaps you can see the flaw in the reasoning:

If my brain is conscious of its own existence, then the universe - which contains my brain, and yours, and everyone else's, plus everything else that may be out there in the rest of the cosmos - must be, by definition, more complex than my little brain. So why would we suppose that THAT is not also conscious of its own existence? Some might say: "Ah, but it's the structure and organisation of the brain that's important. You have neurons that form a network of interconnections so that thoughts can be transmitted and coordinated in various ways and that's what gives rise to the idea that you are a conscious self."

OK, so let's look at the largest picture of the universe that we have so far, from all the Hubble deep field images and the cosmic microwave background and the computer simulations into which we have fed all that data. In 2005, an international team of astrophysicists, the Virgo

Consortium, carried out a simulation called the Millennium Run, which investigated the distribution of matter in the universe and how it evolves over time to form the galaxies we see today. They looked at a volume of space containing twenty million galaxies and dark matter 10 billion billion times the mass of our own sun, and the resulting images took up twenty five Terabytes of storage. Since then, even bigger projects have been carried out and the simulations have given rise to epic videos that are readily available online.

So what do we see? Not the random, homogeneous spread of stars we might have expected from our customary view of the night sky but billions upon billions of galaxies that clump together in clusters and superclusters with strands of stellar material connecting them like a three-dimensional network interspersed with huge voids or empty patches like the holes in a sponge. When you look at these images, you can be excused for experiencing a momentary shiver as you realise that you could be looking down a microscope at a picture of the fine structure of your own brain, in fact many websites offer images of the brain and the universe alongside each other so that you can compare them for yourself. Just type the words "millennium simulation" into your browser and you will have plenty of images and videos to explore.

A universal field of fields, everywhere present - structured in a similar way to a brain and containing all the information that there ever was, is or could be - from which everything arises and to which everything returns and possibly aware of its own existence. Can you think of a better definition of the concept of God?

If that is what the universe is, and we are all part of that, what does that imply?

Like a deer that spends a lifetime searching for the source of a beautiful fragrance without realising that it is smelling its own musk, or the guy travelling the world to seek his fortune while another guy keeps chasing after him to tell him he has won the lottery and is already a rich man, we keep seeking 'out there' what is, and always was, 'in here'.

What if we are the source of what we are seeking? What if what we are looking for is what is doing the looking? What if what is looking at the world through our eyes is God looking at Godself? Wouldn't that be the most empowering idea ever? Wouldn't it be the most liberating idea we ever had?

Strangely, as a species, we seem to find this concept very difficult to accept. Why do you think that is? How did we ever get to take it for granted that the very life force that gave rise to us, the very fabric underlying reality, is somehow separate from us? Why does the statement: "We and God are One" make so many of us feel so uncomfortable? How did we get to the place where voicing such a thought might sound like we were disrespecting the Almighty in some way by entertaining ideas that are way above our station?

What if we are not the insignificant little creatures that we perceive ourselves to be? What if we are one with the entire cosmos and whatever it is that supports and sustains it? What would happen if we were all to realise this now? What if we were all, right now, to fall still and know that we are One? The One.

If people were to remember that they themselves, along with the entire universe, are God, then might they no longer need favoured messengers through which to communicate with the deity? Might their religious leaders become redundant?

This fear seems largely unfounded. Any honest religion capable of reminding people of their own divinity would still have plenty of work to do, because the impression that we are somehow locked into the little region of spacetime enclosed within our own skin is a powerful one.

But a religion can only be honest if its leaders remember its true purpose and have not themselves become so attached to the illusion of separation that they become like the blind leading the blind and begin to consider their own original message to be a kind of blasphemy.

Let's not blame religious leaders, however, since most of us have a vested interest in maintaining the illusion of a separate supreme being, which some people have described to me as their 'cosmic comfort blanket' that they are scared to let go of because it helps make life more bearable. Which is understandable, and fine if people are happy with that.

However, is there any need to 'let go' if the 'something we think we are letting go of' is the something that we actually are? Can an ocean wave, believing itself to be separate from the ocean, let go of the ocean?

Would the act of 'letting go' leave a big, empty, scary hole in which we would be helpless and small and alone, or would it produce a paradigm shift where we realise that we were always alone in the first place but need never feel small and helpless again?

> *"That I am at one with the great being that made me and that formed the galaxies and the universes, etcetera, how did that get taken out of religion? It was not hard."*
>
> *Dr. Michael Ledwith*

Religions as Paths of Love

*"There comes a time in the seeker's life when he discovers
that he is at once the lover and the beloved. The aspiring soul
which he embodies is the lover in him. And the transcendental
Self which he reveals from within is his Beloved."*

Sri Chinmoy

An exercise which has been practiced for millennia is to imagine the
Self as a separate entity and then come to love that entity. We can then
feel, or at least have faith in, the presence of the invisible entity
everywhere. Even when no one else acknowledges or values us, we
can feel valued and loved, yet there is no neediness on our part since
we see the beloved in everything and everyone: every act is an act of
service to the beloved, we work for the welfare of the beloved in all
beings and we keep our attention on the beloved rather than on selfish
personal desires. This practice is at the heart of most of the world's
major religions and the separate, everywhere-present entity, or
Cosmic Consciousness, is usually called 'God'.

*Unable to perceive the shape of you, I find you all around me.
Your presence fills my eyes with your love. It humbles my
heart, for you are everywhere."*

*Attributed to Hakim Sanai and quoted in the film: 'The Shape
of Water'*

There is a purpose to this exercise, though this may be long forgotten.
The purpose is union. When people love each other, they want to be
together. There is a yearning to become one. When a religious devotee
loves their God so much that they yearn to become one with
Him/Her/It, they may take that final step and, out of love, put

111

themselves 'in the shoes of the beloved' and in that moment realise that there was never any separation in the first place. The two become one; or rather the One continues to be One, since there were never two to start with.

"My beloved grows right out of my own heart; how much more union can there be?"

Rumi

There are some lines in religious texts that are very well-known yet often misunderstood. I know that some people take exception to other people quoting from their sacred texts and it is not my intention to offend anyone, however inadvertently, so it is with the greatest respect that I quote these sayings.

An example of a potential misinterpretation is of the words: "Be still and know that I am God." (Psalm 46:10).

When I was a child, I thought that those words came from an old man in the sky, shouting at mere mortals on the ground who were milling around and doing stuff they were not supposed to be doing and getting them to shut up, sit still and pay proper respect to the Boss. In later years I came to realise that the "I am" referred to is neither an elderly bearded guy in the sky nor the disembodied voice of a cosmic being who is separate from us and watching over us to make sure we follow all the rules and punish us if we get it wrong. Is it not possible that the "I am" referred to here is that same "I Am" in all of us and in everything and it is only when we are very still, in body and in mind, that we come to realise this?

Likewise, "I am the light of the world" (John 8:12) does not necessarily suggest that one particular guy is the source of the light, and we should keep following on behind him. Perhaps it means that the " I Am" in all of us and in everything is the source of that light. In fact Matthew 5:14 has it as "You are the light of the world." When we realise this we "will never walk in darkness": of course not, since we are all involved in that process of "shining our light before men, that they may see our good works". We shine a light into every corner by basing all our actions on love, which arises naturally out of the awareness that we are all one.

Knowing this we can understand the advice to "love thy neighbour as thyself" (Matthew 22:39). If we are indeed all one, then our neighbour, along with everyone else and everything else, is part of our universal self and not separate from us. Love is the natural state arising from our recognition of this unity.

Perhaps then, we can come to understand by what was meant by the words: "The kingdom of God is within you." Luke 17:21

"The mysterious kingdom where man may get his best hopes fulfilled is not to be found in future time, as in a next world after death, nor in remote space, as in some region beyond the stars, but here within our own mind and now within our own thought. Such a realization of the mind's innate power to contribute to the making of its own world will raise men – be they saints or cynics – to the level of self-poised sages, calm their minds and soothe their suffering hearts. "

Dr. Paul Brunton

Perhaps we are all the children of God. Perhaps the Father (the universe) gives rise to the Son (all of us) and thereby comes to experience and express itself as the one universal consciousness (or Holy Spirit) that supports and sustains everything.

"Jesus Christ knew he was God. So wake up and find out eventually who you really are. In our culture, of course, they'll say you're crazy and you're blasphemous, and they'll either put you in jail or in a nut house (which is pretty much the same thing). However if you wake up in India and tell your friends and relations, 'My goodness, I've just discovered that I'm God,' they'll laugh and say, 'Oh, congratulations, at last you found out.'"

Alan Watts

Chapter 3 - What the Sages are Telling Us

"Whoever finds the interpretation of these sayings will not experience death.

Jesus said, "Let him who seeks continue seeking until he finds. When he finds, he will become troubled. When he becomes troubled, he will be astonished, and he will rule over the All."

The Gospel of Thomas, Prologue and Verse 2

Throughout recorded history, in all parts of the world, there have lived wise men and women who have left us tantalising snippets of wisdom that hint at a view of reality that is somehow beyond our day to day level of experience.

Some, such as Lao Tse or the Buddha, everyone has heard of, since their words have been published in almost every language for several centuries. Others may be less well known. What is fascinating about all of them is that they are all saying the same thing: we are all one, and it is possible for us to know this.

By 'know', I mean through our own direct experience, rather than as mere information, though of course, like everything in this universe, we are all in-formation.

Going back to matches again, if we think of information as the little bobble on the end of the stick and the sandpaper as experience, when we apply work to put these two elements together, we get the flame that illuminates our darkness: enlightenment. It doesn't matter what type of matches you use, whether they are wooden sticks with pink bobbles or little cardboard things with blue bobbles; it doesn't matter who you are, or where you are or what particular technique you used to strike your match, the flame is the same.

According to our nature, each of us may find that we are attracted to a slightly different 'path' or method of discovering the truth of what we are. Often it is simply that we explore different aspects at different stages in our development. Whatever paths we choose to follow, all lead to the same destination, the top of the same mountain. Whether we refer to it as illumination, enlightenment or self-realisation, it's always the same thing - the awareness that we are all One

At some stage, the shift in perspective that we have spoken of throughout this book may occur. It may be sudden or gradual but, once seen, it changes the way we look at things. Through continuing study, meditation, love and service, we begin to look at the world in a different way. The whole fabric of creation is revealed, either slowly or in a blinding flash of insight. It is as if all the jigsaw pieces have finally fitted together, all the scriptures of the world are self-evident. We may even discover that it was the idea that we were on some kind of path that was actually holding us back.

The idea of a path or journey implies that there is somewhere to go: from here to there, from now to then. But what if there is nowhere you need to go? What if everything you need is right here, right now? What if the very idea of following a path is the thing that prevents you from seeing what you already are? What if you are already perfect, just as you are?

Strictly speaking, no "paths" are necessary. We are all life. We are all one. There is nothing else to know.

For some of us it might take many years before the penny drops. For others it might be very quick. It could be now.

As Sogyal Rinpoche said: "Once you have the view, you will be like the sky: empty, spacious and pure from the beginning". And it's the same view for all of us. When you see it, you know that what you are seeing is the same as it was for all those wise people who have spoken about it for millennia; you recognise it in their words.

So what advice have these men and women, from ancient sages to present day wisdom holders, passed on to us in order to help us to realise the truth for ourselves?

When we begin to look for such advice, we find lots of it! Entire systems have been developed for the purpose of enabling us to overcome our sense of separation and return to the awareness of unity.

Yoga, for example, is not just a physical exercise system but includes many other practices designed to wake us up, from the pursuit of knowledge and wisdom to selfless action, service to others, devotion and unity. The word 'yoga' means 'union', and the ultimate yoga teaching is the 'pathless path' of Advaita, 'not two', which reminds us that the individual self and the universal Self are not two separate things: there is only the One, as there always was and always will be.

Such wisdom traditions are not confined to India but are found across the globe from the Taoist sages and Shaolin monks of China to the Sufi mystics of the Middle East and the shamans of Hawaii.

When we study the words of the wise, from ancient sages to modern scientists, we find the same message, over and over again.

So it's time now for me to sit back and let some of the world's great teachers speak for themselves.

"What appears and disappears, is not real.
The seer remains.
Now, find out who the seer is."

Ramana Maharshi

"You live in illusions and the appearance of things.
There is a Reality.
You are that Reality.
When you recognise this you will realise that you are no thing
and being no thing, you are everything."

Kalu Rinpoche (Twentieth century Tibetan Buddhist)

"Life is a visible state among the invisible."

The Bhagavad Gita

"As a million sparks rise from a single fire, separate and
come together again as they fall back into it...So inanimate
and live creation emerges from God's form, and since they
arise from him they will return again."

Guru Nanak

"All that man has here externally in multiplicity is intrinsically One. Here all blades of grass, wood and stone, all things are One. This is the deepest depth..."

Meister Eckhart

"All creatures are the same life, the same essence, the same power, the same one and nothing less."

Henry Suso

"The reason why our thinking ego is met nowhere within our scientific world picture (is) because it is itself that world picture. It is identical with the whole and therefore cannot be contained in it as a part of it... the overall number of minds is just one... The world extended in space and time is but our representation. Experience does not give us the slightest clue of its being anything besides that."

Erwin Schroedinger, The Oneness of Mind

"Whether you are going or staying or sitting or lying down, the whole world is your own self...Suddenly one day everything is empty like space which has no inside or outside, no bottom or top, and you are aware of the one principle pervading all the ten thousand things. You know then that your heart is so vast that it can never be measured. 'Heaven and Earth and I of one root; the thousand things and I are one body.' These words are of burning import and absolutely true...When you come to grasp it, you find it was ever before your eyes."

Daikaku, From 'Zen and the Ways' by Trevor Leggett

"Wherever you are, you are one with the clouds and one with the sun and the stars you see. You are one with everything. That is more true than I can say, and more true than you can hear...Wherever I go, I meet myself."

Shunryu Suzuki

"In looking out upon the world, we forget that the world is looking at itself."

"You yourself are the eternal energy which appears as this universe. You didn't come into this world, you came out of it. Like a wave from the ocean... as leaves from a tree. As the ocean "waves," the Universe "peoples." Every individual is an expression of the whole realm of Nature, a unique action of the total Universe."

Alan Watts

"There is no greater mystery than this, that we keep seeking reality though in fact we are reality."

Ramana Maharshi

"Let the waves of the Universe rise and fall as they will You have nothing to gain or lose. You are the Ocean."

Ashtavakra Gita

"If I am to know God directly, I must become completely God, and God I, so that this God and this I become one I."

Meister Eckhart.

"The ten thousand things and I are one.
We are already one –
What else is there to say?"

Chuang Tzu

In our quest for enlightenment, the sages advise us to ask questions rather than to follow blindly; to be kind, to be loving and to generally look after our planet and each other to the best of our ability, and the main tool they recommend to us for becoming self-realised in this lifetime is the practice of meditation. So let's have a closer look at that.

Meditation

"My teaching is simple: sit and be."

Buddha Maitreya

Meditation is the process of bringing the mind to a state in which it rests quietly, thoughts settle and dissolve away and there is simply a sense of being fully present in the moment: alert, awake and yet deeply at peace.

Sounds easy doesn't it? Yet when we first attempt to sit down and clear the mind of all thoughts, the mind has different ideas. Literally! Random thoughts bubble up out of nowhere, like those irritating pop-up menus that appear on your computer screen and invite you to click on them, which of course just pulls you further in so that they now fill the whole screen with full-colour images and either try to get you to buy something or mess up your machine so it can't function properly.

So what do we do with pop-up menus? Ignore them! We just focus on the background instead. It's the same with thoughts. If we don't pay them any attention, they tend to fade away.

As we begin to allow the mind to settle, it can be helpful to see all distractions, such as external sounds or internal thoughts, as ripples on the surface of an ocean or as musical vibrations on the surface of the silence. You can be aware of all the waving yet choose to rest in the deepest depths.

You can't lose yourself by emptying your mind of clutter, you just become more yourself: your real self, rather than a bunch of random ideas.

You are not your thoughts, you are the owner of your brain, the master of your mind, the witness of all the stuff that goes on in there.

Ignoring the passing show of thoughts, however, can be easier said than done. It's a bit like trying to pull yourself up off the floor with your own shoelaces: the harder you try not to think, the more you end up thinking about not thinking. The more you try to push thoughts out of your head, the more they will stick around and annoy you, enthused by all the attention they are getting.

The Sage and the Donkey

A young man heard that a famous wise man was passing through the area. Eager to be accepted as a disciple, he followed the old man and caught up with him beside a stream where he had paused to let his donkey have a drink.

"Please," begged the young man. "Let me travel with you and be your disciple. There is nothing I want more than to become enlightened, as you are, and to live as you do. I will do anything you ask."

"OK," replied the sage. "I will rest here for a few days. Go home and come back to me one week from now. During the week, I have only one instruction for you to follow and that is this: do not think about this donkey."

The young man looked at the grey donkey drinking peacefully in the shallow water and resolved that he would not think about this animal at all during the coming week. "This is easy!" he thought. "Such a simple task and I will become a student of this great master." So he thanked the old man profusely and went home.

A week later, as the sage rolled up his blanket and prepared to move on, the young man returned.

"Well?" he inquired pleasantly. "Did you do what I asked?"

"I tried." The young man admitted sadly. "But I must confess that the harder I tried the more I thought of the donkey. I thought about him night and day. I even dreamed about the donkey. I have failed your test and I am not worthy to become your disciple."

"Ha!" said the sage. "An honest student! And you have learned your first lesson well. You are welcome to accompany me on my journey."

So as well as describing a process and a state of mind, the word 'meditation' is also used to describe a wide range of practices that can help you to get around this difficulty and overcome the natural tendency of the mind to keep offering you little snippets to divert your attention from the task in hand and cause you to wander off into yet another daydream. Meditation techniques can be thought of as helpful ways to trick the mind into being still.

How meditation works

"Our essential nature is usually overshadowed by the activity of the mind. When the mind has settled, we are established in our essential nature which is unbounded consciousness."

The Yoga Sutras of Patanjali

To keep the mind happy and make it shut up, we start by giving it something to do, something simple such as watching the breathing or listening to the silence behind the sounds, or staring at a candle flame or the sparkling reflections of sunlight on water, or repeating a mantra – a word or short phrase that you either chant aloud or simply listen to in your mind.

It's entirely up to you which technique you decide to use. It's best if it's something you have chosen yourself, something that feels right for you. That way, you're more likely to stick with it and give it time to work for you.

Whatever you choose to focus on, you just rest your attention lightly on it and follow it through any distractions that arise around you or inside your head, until all the other stuff settles down like mud in water and your mind becomes clear and steady; at which point, you can just let go of the mantra or whatever, and simply allow yourself to be fully present in the moment.

"When water is still it is like a mirror...and if water thus derives lucidity from stillness, how much more the faculties of the mind? The mind of the sage, being in repose, becomes the mirror of the universe."

Chuang Tzu

124

How long that peace lasts will vary. Sometimes several minutes may pass before another thought pops into the space, sometimes just a few seconds. That's all perfectly normal. It's the same for most people. You don't have to achieve anything. You can't be 'good at' or 'bad at' meditation. It just is what it is, so simply observe and let it be and don't expect too much. If your head is full of random ideas and glorious HD full-colour images and you start to think that you are 'failing' in some way at this whole meditation thing, just look at all that stuff in your mind for a moment. You can see it, right there. So what is doing the looking?

Meditation is not about glorious visions, psychic powers or heavenly choruses, though your imagination may happily oblige if you are looking for such things. The meditative state is very ordinary in many ways: a quietness that is entirely unremarkable because it is always there and always has been there, underlying all the surface stuff. That's why it's so often overlooked. Yet once you come to recognise it, you will find that there is nothing more profound.

There is a famous Zen story about a young monk who bursts into his master's room to announce that he has just seen a brilliant vision of a golden Buddha. The master doesn't even look up as he tells the student: "Don't worry. If you keep practicing, it will go away."

Your sense of time might shift a bit so that what seems to be a few minutes was actually half an hour. Even a few seconds of meditative peace may be enough to refresh you deeply and leave you feeling more steady and in control. You may find that you feel a sense of contentment and inner quietness that carries over into whatever you are doing in your life and makes everything that little bit easier for you to manage. You might even experience a sense of flow, in which some tasks seem almost effortless, as if they are doing themselves while you look on and watch. If not, that's fine too. There is no right or wrong, no success or failure. Just have a go from time to time and allow yourself to be at ease with yourself.

You can just be present in the moment, noticing any thoughts and feelings without judgement or any attempt to fix them, understand them or do anything in particular about them; you can simply accept them as interesting, yet temporary, experiences and gently let them go, the way that tiny clouds may arise and dissolve back into a perfect sky, and then return your attention to the 'sky' and come fully to rest in the quiet space underlying all thought.

You don't need to spend hours or days practicing meditation. Twenty minutes a day is fine. Attempting to keep your mind empty for days or weeks at a time is overkill and likely to make you feel cut off from reality. It may even lead to lots of rumination, introspection and self-analysis that messes up your mental health and well-being. When practiced in moderation, however, meditation is likely to improve your ability to think clearly, deepen your understanding of reality and increase your sense of connectedness to everything. You are likely to feel serene, alert and able to sleep more deeply at night.

As well as improving our mental and emotional well-being, improving our powers of concentration and perhaps enabling the shift in world view that brings about our enlightenment, meditation has also been shown to improve our physical health by reducing inflammation in the body, thus reducing the risk of illnesses ranging from heart disease and rheumatoid arthritis to Alzheimer's disease and cancer. It also appears to lengthen our telomeres - the end tips of DNA that protect our genetic material - thereby increasing our life expectancy. When it has been taught in schools, children have become calmer and able to learn more effectively. In cities, as more people begin to practice meditation, crime rates have been shown to decrease.

No wonder, then, that people who meditate seem to be generally happier.

"When, through the practice of yoga, the mind ceases its restless movements and becomes still, one realizes the Self. It satisfies one entirely. Then one knows that infinite happiness which can be realized by the purified heart but is beyond the grasp of the senses."

The Bhagavad Gita

What meditation is not

As the yoga master, Sadhguru, says: learning to meditate does not involve the amazing skill of *falling asleep* while sitting upright in a vertical position! You may, however, find that you sleep more easily and deeply when you have practiced meditation for a while. Nor does it involve the kind of *mental blankness* you get when you are feeling dazed or totally 'out of it'. In the meditative state, you are wide awake, fully alert and present in the moment.

Meditation is not *guided imagery* or *visualisation*. There is a lot to be said for imagining yourself to be in some beautiful setting such as a tropical beach or a forest glade, where you can relax and enjoy the scenery. It's a great way to fully unwind and perhaps get off to sleep and many therapists use such imagery to enable people to reduce anxiety and gain a fresh perspective on life. So it's brilliant in many ways; it's just not meditation because, whenever you are visualising something, the mind is still active rather than resting in stillness and peace.

Meditation is also not the same as *contemplation*. In the meditative state, there are no thoughts, whereas contemplation is 'about' something. In contemplation, we may allow the mind to explore a

127

particular subject, challenge or problem and then let it go while we rest quietly, or meditate, or go for a walk, or get on with something else. What may happen then is that some kind of insight or solution may arise quite naturally from a deeper part of the mind, as inspiration or intuition. Although meditation and contemplation are not the same thing, the discipline gained through meditation practice may make contemplation easier.

> *"A person who does not meditate cannot have wisdom. He may be able to concentrate, but not for any length of time. His power of concentration remains weak and cannot be maintained."*

> *Rabbi Nachman*

Meditation is not a *trance state*, the definition of which is a state of locked attention: a kind of tunnel vision in which we are focussed on one thing and shutting out all the rest. Whether you choose to meditate with your eyes open or closed, even though your mind is still, your attention is wide open and very alert to everything, in all directions. In this way, the meditative state is the opposite of a trance state. With practice, you can develop the ability to mentally step back, rest in the stillness underlying everything and open the awareness outwards in any situation. The practical advantages of this are significant. In everyday life, the habit of stepping back, calming down and taking a wider viewpoint helps you to think more clearly, avoid excessive emotional arousal and develop a greater ability to see other people's points of view.

Perhaps most importantly, meditation is not *rumination* or *introspection*. We may believe ourselves to be meditating on a problem when we are actually going over and over things in our mind, analysing and worrying, which can lead to disturbed sleep patterns, anxiety and depression. In general, meditation is not about past memories or future concerns, it's about resting in this present moment, right now, with nothing to do, nothing to achieve: only pure awareness of being.

"In this quietness falls down the burden of all your sorrows."

The Bhagavad Gita

The words meditation and *mindfulness* are often used interchangeably but again, they are not the same thing. Mindfulness is simply a word used to describe being consciously present in the moment rather than engaging in thoughts about the past or the future. It could be called an awareness of what is happening right now, rather than having the mind full of thoughts and ideas. Since most of our day to day worries tend to be about things that happened in the past or things we fear might happen in the future, just being in the present moment for a while can be a blessed relief.

"The more you talk and think about it, the further astray you wander from the truth. Stop talking and thinking, and there is nothing you will not be able to know."

Zen Master

In modern societies, we tend to over-value the practice of multi-tasking, with workers barely allowed time to clear their desks before another load is heaped on their shoulders. However, this may be counter-productive, leading to stress, illness and lots of loose ends slipping. When we have the time to give each job our full attention, for its own sake, without being too wrapped up in thoughts about the results, we are likely to do each one properly and get through it faster than when our attention was being dragged in several directions at once. We can just do each task in the moment, to the best of our ability, and then let it go and get on with something else.

Even in unpleasant situations, being present may help us to remain calm and do whatever needs to be done. When, while working as a game warden in my youth, I found myself face to face with a fully grown male lion, a focus on my likely imminent demise might have resulted in a less than favourable outcome. I was lucky: he walked away and didn't see fit to terminate my writing career at that point!

Any job you do, from painting a picture to handling an emergency, requires presence, as does the appreciation of beauty in your surroundings or the ability to listen to what someone is saying to you.

They said to him, "Tell us who you are, so that we may believe in you." He said to them, "You read the face of the sky and of the earth, but you have not recognised the one who is before you and do not know how to read this moment."

The Gospel of Thomas, Verse 91

This doesn't mean that you should spend every moment of every day in a state of perfect mindfulness. People who have suffered brain injuries resulting in the loss of their long-term memory have an unenviable existence living in a perpetual now. The ability to focus on the present, while retaining access to memories of the past and plans for the future, provides us with a context in which we can learn, progress and engage effectively with reality, so again moderation is the key, as with any spiritual practice.

Our response to the now becomes our future. We can choose what we stand for and so shape what we become. We can create a vision of how we want the world to be and, from this, we can prioritise the tasks in hand and then do one thing at a time and give each one our full attention.

Although mindfulness is not the same as meditation, it is a prerequisite for it. You can't meditate if your attention is wrapped up in past or future concerns: you need to be present in order to focus on whatever meditative technique you decide to use and to notice the quiet mind, prior to noticing the noticing!

> *"Meditation is a pure, scientific method. In science you call it observation, observation of the objects. When you move inwards it is the same observation just taking a one-hundred-and eighty-degree turn and looking in. That's what we call meditation. No god is needed, no Bible is needed. You need not have a belief system as prerequisite. An atheist can meditate, just as anybody else can, because meditation is only a method of turning inwards."*
>
> *- Osho*

Two Simple Meditation Techniques

For both of these, simply sit still in a comfortable, upright position, either on the floor or in a chair, preferably somewhere quiet, where you are unlikely to be disturbed.

Begin by taking a deep breath, holding it for a moment and then exhaling with a deep sigh. As you do this, allow it to release any tensions in your body and simply let go. Let your shoulders drop and your thighs flop and observe the weight of your body sinking downwards towards the floor while still supported by your upright spine.

A Meditation on Breathing

As long as we are alive, our breathing is available to us as a meditational tool. It has been doing its thing quite happily since the day we were born, even when we haven't been paying it any attention. Just watching it quietly from time to time, while it gets on with its business, can be very valuable to us as a method of bringing the mind to stillness.

With the body settled and comfortable, become aware that it is breathing. Lightly rest the attention on the breath and feel the air entering and leaving the body. Don't try to do anything to alter the rhythm or depth of the breathing. It may become slower or faster, deeper or more shallow; simply observe what it does very naturally, all by itself.

If you like, you can attempt to notice the point where the in-breath becomes the out-breath, or the point where the out-breath becomes the in-breath. Or maybe you can imagine the air as a golden circle coming in through your nose as you inhale and out through a point on your lower abdomen, just below your navel, then traveling upwards to your nose again. The idea is to simply give your mind something to focus on.

If there are any distractions, or you become aware that your mind has wandered off into various thoughts, as soon as you notice that, just gently refocus your attention on the breathing. Be kind to yourself. It's not a competition. And it gets easier with practice.

Eventually, you can just let go and come fully to rest in the stillness underlying everything.

Watching the breathing can also be useful in times of stress, such as before an exam or a job interview or if you find yourself dealing with an emergency or you are about to give a public speech or performance.

In such situations, it can be helpful to allow just a little bit more time for the out breath. This can allow your heart rate to settle, bring your rational mind back online and allow you to give your best in that situation. You may be amazed at your own capabilities.

A Meditation on Silence

Even in a crowded city with noises around you, if you listen very carefully, you can be aware of the silence behind the sounds. The mind has a natural tendency to flit from sound to sound and offer various full-colour images of what might be producing each of them, but we don't have to get caught up in that imagery.

As you sit quietly and comfortably in whatever place you have chosen for your meditation, let the hearing go right out and just listen. Can you listen to birdsong without wondering what kind of bird produced it? Can you let a conversation continue in the next room without attempting to hear what is being said or identify who is speaking? Can you be open to the sound of traffic without conjuring up images of passing cars? Simply listen and let all of that wash over you like ripples playing on the surface of a pond while your mind rests in the deepest depths of the silence that underlies it: quiet, tranquil and perfectly still.

An Exercise in Mindfulness

Try sitting for a few minutes in a park or a garden. Just rest in the beauty of your surroundings and experience it fully with all your senses. You don't need to label any experience or sense-impression. You don't need to selectively overlook the litter bin and focus preferentially on the flowers. A dirty rag in the gutter is no less worthy of your attention than the smell of freshly cut grass. Just be there with it all and let it be. Perhaps there may be a timelessness about it and the world may seem richer and more alive.

"The time of business does not with me differ from the time of prayer, and in the noise and clutter of my kitchen while several people are at the same time calling for different things, I possess God in as great a tranquillity as if I were on my knees at the blessed sacrament."

Brother Lawrence

Part 2 – Returning To The Centre

"Awaken by closing the eyes. See the light within."

L. Ryokan

Chapter 4 - Where Are You Coming From?

How much sense these words make will depend on how you see the world at this time. Whatever is happening in your life right now, the perspective you gain from reading this book may be of some value to you, though some situations may make that trickier than others.

If you are struggling to stay alive in a hostile environment, or trying to find food and shelter for yourself and your family, you will undoubtedly be looking at this information from a different angle than if you are languishing in an infinity pool on your own tropical island. You may not have the spare capacity to even begin to think about what you can do for others if you are currently weighed down by your own problems and concerns. Even enormous wealth does not guarantee that people will be happy. Rich or poor, if you are suffering from depression, anxiety, grief, loneliness, fear, anger or any of the other unhelpful conditions that appear to beset most of us at some stage in our lives, then the idea of saving our species and our world may seem impossible or inappropriate for you.

Whatever your current circumstances, however, the way you are looking at the world may be having a powerful influence on the way you are feeling and the amount of benefit you are able to derive from this book.

How Our World-view Shapes Our World

We each have our own unique world-view, our own take on reality, because of the mental maps we scan the world through.

One of our most powerful mental maps is the one that consists of our personal answer to the question of "What am I?" Our personal take on this one affects everything we do: how we feel about ourselves, how we relate to others and how we live our lives. Ultimately, it can affect the future survival of our species.

If, for example, we had a world-view that went something along the lines of: "The universe is a cold, empty, meaningless place, life is an accident, I am as small and helpless as a gnat and my life is meaningless, so I might as well either end it all now or get what I can for myself, whether or not it causes harm to anyone else, because their lives are also meaningless and we're all going to die anyway", we could not be terribly surprised if we found ourselves depressed, unpopular and possibly in prison.

Compare that with the view taken by someone who says: "I'm constantly amazed at the miracle of life, the beauty of the world we live in and the way everything is interconnected. I think the greatest miracle of all is the love between people and I want to do everything I can to look after this world and make others happy. That's what my life is about."

Does that last one seem a bit cheesy and too good to be true? We could think: "It's all very well for that second person to be so goody-goody. They probably had all the breaks: rich parents, good education, good job. It's easy to say life is brilliant when you have an easy ride. The other poor soul probably had all the crap thrown at them!"

It's possible. But supposing those two people had lived through exactly the same set of circumstances - the same parents, opportunities, wealth and all the rest of it – and yet they still saw the world in very different ways. How is that possible? Can we choose to change our view of the world, whatever our circumstances, in the same way that we can put on a different pair of spectacles?

Ripples

If you are in a difficult situation right now, maybe you can find some comfort or inner strength here to help you to endure. Perhaps you might feel better equipped to reduce your own burden a little after reading this book. Or perhaps someone else who has read this book will feel more motivated to help you in a time of need.

Maybe two people, after reading these words, will help each other and both will benefit. Witnessing this, maybe a whole community will benefit and set an example for a nation to follow. Perhaps that nation will become an inspiring role model for the whole world. None of us can know the consequences that can ripple outwards from a simple act of kindness or courage that, in turn, arose from a recognition of unity. In the words of a poem I wrote many years ago:

The work of any man
Is like a ripple in a pond.
He cannot cure the whole world's ills,
Or wave a magic wand.
The place where he is standing
Is the point where he must start.
Alone in his small corner,
He may strive to play his part.
With kindness and compassion
He may live and love and be,
And so set an example
For the few who choose to see,
And if they choose to follow
They may play their parts in turn

And set their own examples
So that other men might learn.
The wisdom of a man thus spreads
Unto the farthest shore,
Like ripples flowing outwards
To be felt for evermore.

Tolerance

You may wonder how it is possible to get on well with everyone, let alone be kind or compassionate, when so many people are mean, hateful, spiteful and hostile. How can you love a criminal, a terrorist or even some of the unpleasant folks you meet on a day to day basis? I found myself asking this question back in 1984, when the Yorkshire Ripper was at large and had just claimed his thirteenth victim, a university student like myself at that time. How could anyone not hate him?

The answer, surprisingly, came to me after the birth of my first child. As I looked at my dear little baby, I would wonder what she might be like at six months old, or ten years old, or as an adult. Then suddenly it hit me! I wondered what the Yorkshire Ripper might have been like as a baby!

In that moment, it was as if a lead weight around my shoulders had fallen away. There was no more hatred. That hatred had been screwing me up, now it was gone. How can anyone hate a baby? What had happened to that tiny, innocent child to make him turn out the way he did? Was he unfortunate enough to have inherited bad genes, or to experience dreadful things during his life? I had no way of knowing, but the hatred had gone, not just for him, but for everyone!

I would walk down the street, looking at each person I passed by and wondering what they might have been like as a newborn. I felt a bit like the mother of every person on the planet. I saw that, while terrible behaviour and acts of violence cannot be tolerated, and some people may need to be locked away for everyone else's safety, hatred is pointless and damaging to society and to our own sanity. I wondered how the world might be if we were all to look at each other and see the innocent children we once were.

I discovered that living a life without hating anyone is liberating. I felt lighter, more free and more connected to other people and I found myself smiling more and receiving more smiles in return. Situations that I might, at one time, have found awkward or intimidating often became easier to deal with when approached with a little more empathy and compassion.

An Exercise on Freedom from Hatred

You might like to try this for yourself. Just start by imagining the next person you meet as a newly-born baby. And the next person...and the next...

Try it with a few people you have found difficult to get on with.

Is there any particular group of people that you have felt antipathy towards, for religious, racial, political, cultural or any other reasons? Try it with them.

There is no 'you and me' or 'us and them': we are one family and we need to help each other. Ultimately, we need to evolve to the point where we can concern ourselves with supporting each other through any of the inevitable natural disasters that occur on our planet, without compounding our problems by adding wars, poverty, and other man-made hardships to the mix of tribulations that we face. Our greatest evolutionary imperative is surely to discover our true humanity, and the human race can perhaps be seen as our race to become fully human in time to save ourselves and our world.

Perhaps, before we go on, you might like to try the following exercises.

Exercises on the Oneness of Humanity

At the beginning of this book, we asked ourselves the question: "What was I before I was even given a name?"

Let's go a bit further with our questioning.

First Exercise:

What were you ten minutes ago, when a completely different set of thoughts occupied your mind?

How about ten years ago? Who were you then?

Who were you before you reached your present height and weight? Not how tall were you then or how much did you weigh at that time but who was the deep down you that was experiencing your life back in those days?

Second Exercise:

Next, think about the country of your birth - its people, its customs and its culture. The people who raised you. Their beliefs and values.

Now think of a country very different from yours, perhaps a few thousand miles away, on the other side of the world. What kind of culture exists there? What kinds of beliefs do a majority of the people who were born in that country hold? Imagine if you had been born there. What might that have been like? Imagine being yourself, yet born and raised in that country, being visited by the present you.

Imagine getting on a plane and going to that other country and meeting the you that was born over there. Would you know yourself?

Would you recognise the same self that was looking out through different eyes and a layer of different memories, different values, different thoughts?

Would you be able to say "It's OK. I know you. I am you."? Or would you dismiss that person as foreign, alien, different, because of their different experiences or the colour of their skin?

What if you had been born into a body that was of a different gender to the one you currently find yourself in?

Third Exercise:

Now imagine that reincarnation is a thing (you don't have to believe it, just imagine, for the purposes of this exercise). Imagine that, every time we die, we come back again as someone else. Imagine that this can happen an infinite number of times and that you have already been every person in history and every person currently living on this planet.

Now walk down a busy street and look at every person you meet as if you are looking at yourself in a past life.

There are computer games such as the Harry Potter series in which you can play the whole thing as Harry and then, when it's 'game over,' you can choose to start again as Harry again, or as Hermione or Ron. If we live within a computer simulation, perhaps our real Self gets to play out this game of life through different characters and what I call 'me' is just the avatar I chose to wear on this particular occasion.

"You are not a little human playing at being Big G.
You are Big G playing at being a human - and everything else."

Alan Watts

In a moment, we will look at an empowering model that, when combined with the skill of meditation, may enable us to cope with the inevitable pressures of life and have the spare capacity required to work together in creating a better world and safeguarding it for the next generation.

However, we also need to be very clear about how to tame and use another gift we were given at birth, a powerful tool that can make us or break us: our imagination.

Imagination: a Double-edged Sword

"Imagination is more important than knowledge. For knowledge is limited, whereas imagination embraces the entire world, stimulating progress, giving birth to evolution. It is, strictly speaking, a real factor in scientific research."

Albert Einstein

Every worthwhile creation produced by human beings began as an idea in someone's mind. From bridges to palaces, from paintings to symphonies, all the great works of art and architecture, and even the greatest discoveries of science, began as ideas in somebody's head. Einstein, a man whose far-reaching insights into the relativity of time and space began by imagining riding on a sunbeam, told us that imagination is more important than knowledge. He saw knowledge as limiting us to what we already know, which may seem to be quite a lot but is actually very little compared with what there is yet to be learned. Through the power of our imagination, we can go to the ends of the universe or the depths of the atom or indeed ride on a photon at the speed of light.

If we are to become enlightened as a result of this 'quest' of ours, any insights will be glimpsed in our 'mind's eye', using the power of our imagination, and if we are to create a better and safer world, it will be because there are people alive today who are able to visualise what such a world could be like and how to make it a reality.

Imagination, then, is a wonderful thing: a capacity which defines us as human beings but, like any tool, it can be used or it can be misused. Using our imagination to focus on ideas that benefit ourselves and our world is a helpful pursuit, but if we spend a disproportionate amount of time with our focus on worst-case scenarios and dark and scary images, it will happily oblige us as we literally scare ourselves to death!

If we use our imagination to conjure up the wealth and possessions we feel we are entitled to, or to justify our resentment of those who have more and refuse to share it with us, or to focus on seeking creative ways to rid ourselves of those whom we perceive to have wronged us, the world we create will be an uncomfortable and unforgiving place. If we over-use our imagination to visualise perceived threats, we may even end up with a self-imposed prison sentence that prevents us from venturing outside our own houses and causes us to become totally reliant on others to meet even our most basic needs.

If we are to work together to save our world from destruction, much will depend on our ability and willingness to use our imagination in positive ways to maintain a helpful world-view and engage effectively with reality.

The Bubble

Imagine that you are standing inside a huge glass bubble. Painted on the glass, there are lots of dots of different colours. If you were to stand with your eye up against a black spot, the whole world outside the bubble would look black. If you stood back a bit and glimpsed some of the other colours available, you could maybe choose a nice rose-tinted one, or perhaps avoid the dots and look through the clear bits of glass. You might even find a way of washing off all the dots and enjoying a completely unobstructed, all-round view, or even smashing the glass and being totally free.

The Wall

When you feel as if there is a wall in front of you that you can't get through and you seem to spend a lot of time beating your head against it, you may find that, if you step back a little, you can see that it's only shoulder-width wide and you can just walk around it. An overly-emotional brain limits our choices. Hungry, stressed dogs on one side of a fence will keep trying to get through it to food on the other side and not see a gap in the fence that is obvious to them when they are not hungry.

The Mountain

When we are upset, we can build ourselves a 'mountain of misery' that seems enormous when our noses are up against it. Stepping back, we see that it's just a molehill. In years to come, we may look back and wonder why we ever made such a fuss about it.

Whichever analogy works best for you, you can see that the way out of the doldrums tends to depend on your ability to mentally step back and see the wider picture – an ability that can be trained through the practice of meditation. In addition, although the human brain is incredibly complex, it is useful to have a clear and simple outline of how it works in order to be able to use it well and so improve our chances of living a happy and meaningful life and perhaps becoming 'enlightened' in the process. The most useful model I have come across, in this respect, is the APET model.

Chapter 5 – The Obedient Brain

*"What a liberation to realize that the 'voice in my head' is not
who I am. Who am I then? The one who sees that."*

~ Eckhart Tolle

The APET Model

The APET model is a way of looking at how the human mind works.
Developed by Joe Griffin and Ivan Tyrell of the Human Givens
Institute, it is extremely empowering because it allows us to get a
handle on what goes on inside our own heads. Many of the day-to-day
skills we can learn, such as how to cheer ourselves up, control our
temper, keep our cool in a crisis and get a decent grip on reality
generally, are tied in to this.

The best way that I have found to explain the APET model is by
telling a story. I am not the first to use such metaphors when
describing the workings of the brain. Others have used them to great
effect, including Griffin and Tyrell, especially in their book *Freedom
From Addiction*, and John Ratey, in *A User's Guide to the Brain*. The
following is my own personal interpretation, after which we'll have a
look at what this means in terms of the structure of the brain and what
scientists currently know about how the mind works. You'll then see
what the letters APET stand for and how this model can be useful to
us by allowing us to control our own thoughts and emotions, rather
than having them control us.

The Company

*In a busy city, there was a large building, the headquarters of a very
successful and long-established business. Within the company, the
owner employed just a few members of staff: a manager, a secretary*

146

and two security guards. The secretary had access to an enormous database and the manager had access to a powerful computer which could solve very complicated problems. The security guards each had an app on their phone which scanned photos of anyone who had visited before and used facial recognition software to pull up a file telling them whether any new visitors were likely to be helpful or dangerous.

When anyone arrived at the front doors, the security guards would compare the visitor with all the available images. If there was not an exact match, they would see which photo the new visitor was most like. They would then quickly send a message to the secretary, together with an emotional tag as an indication of the threat level they perceived. The secretary would do a search on the database to see what else was stored there that might be useful in the assessment of the newcomer and then send all the relevant details up to the boss (manager), along with a post-it note describing the overall 'feeling' as to the potential helpfulness or threat level of the situation.

The boss, armed with all this information, would then deal with the visitor appropriately and solve any problems that arose, using the super-computer.

Of course, the company had emergency systems in place, just in case anything extreme occurred, and this had saved them from many previous threats and challenges. When danger threatened, the security guards would recognise the seriousness of the situation and, rather than waste time telling the boss, they and the secretary would deal with it on their own and then let the boss know what had happened as soon as the danger had passed.

This procedure worked very well, which is why the company was so successful. The owner could generally leave it in the capable hands of the team and go off on holiday for long periods while they got on with it - until a certain day when something went wrong.

On that day there was a major incident. It was the worst emergency the team had ever dealt with, and although the company survived, something was different. The secretary was traumatised and spent a lot of time trawling through the database to try to work out how it had happened and make sure it couldn't happen again. The security guards were duly informed that now all visitors were to be considered to be a potential threat and only to let in large amounts of ice cream and chocolate. The secretary was now far too busy to tell the boss about what was going on, so the boss assumed that everything was fine, and had a good rest.

Business declined rapidly and the arrival of any visitor triggered a major security alert that confirmed the secretary's suspicions that the world was a dangerous and hostile place and they should shut down all operations until the coast was clear. The manager slept on, blissfully unaware of this spiral into decline.

Then, fortunately, the owner came back from holiday!

If you were the owner, what would you have done? Close the company and give up? Fire all the staff and get in some new people who knew what they were doing?

The owner actually decided to help the secretary to calm down. The secretary, feeling calmer and more in control now, decided to let the boss know what was going on. The boss woke up, used the big computer to assess the situation, supplied the guards with a more accurate set of photos and ordered the storerooms to be cleaned and emptied of ice cream and chocolate. Business picked up and the company once again became successful.

How the Brain Works

The above story is of course a metaphor for a human being. It provides us with a useful representation of how our brain deals with information.

The visitors in the story represent incoming information via the senses (the front door). The security guards are the amygdalae: two walnut-sized structures, one on each side of the brain. They are responsible for screening that incoming information, comparing it with our existing mental maps and finding an exact or partial 'fit' to describe it. This is called 'pattern-matching'. So if we eat a new fruit, we tend to say something like: "It looks like a grape, it tastes a bit like a strawberry but it smells more like an orange."

The amygdalae then pass the message on to the limbic system, together with an emotional tag – varying amounts of neurotransmitters such as dopamine - to say whether it might be helpful or threatening. The limbic system trawls the memory bank for any extra information and then offers the lot up to the rational higher cortex where a decision is made about what, if anything, to do with the new information.

There is, therefore, a time delay between the limbic system (the secretary) getting the message and the frontal lobes or higher cortex (the boss) getting to know about what's going on.

We can summarise this sequence of events like this:

A - P - E - T

A = Activating Event (The visitor)

P = Pattern Matching (The Security Guards)

E = Emotions (The Secretary)

T = Rational Thinking (The Boss)

To this, we can also add a further letter:

S = The Observing Self (The Owner)

In the West, some of the most successful psychotherapy ever devised has been developed over the past few decades, based on this insight: that although our thoughts do affect our emotions, they do not always precede our emotions; in fact the emotions often come first and sometimes even prevent us from accessing our rational thought processes at all.

For example, we may become angry without intending to do so or even understanding why we feel that way. It is only at the point where we see that anger has already arisen that we have the opportunity to choose our response. Inmates at a local prison found this information invaluable and told us that, had they known about the APET model years ago, they might never have committed the crimes that led to their incarceration.

While this model may appear to be overly simplistic, it is memorable and usable and it follows on from the work of scientists such as Paul MacLean, who studied in great detail how emotions arise in the brain and how they affect our thinking. In the East, where meditation has been practiced for centuries and an understanding of the mind has always been a valued pursuit, similar models have long been available.

As in the story, some situations are just too pressing for all this rigmarole to take place. For example, if there is a train hurtling towards you and you are standing on the track, a good idea would be to get the heck off the track before it hits you. Because of the time delay between any message getting from the emotional brain (limbic system) to the rational brain (higher cortex), the higher cortex just doesn't have time to get involved in this decision, calculating trajectories and so forth. If it did, the story would end right there. Period.

Fortunately for us, in such a situation there is a chance that the security guards and secretary can get us off the track very quickly on their own and only let the boss know a bit later on, when we are out of harm's way and the train has passed us by. So we may not become fully conscious of what is going on until after the event. We usually call this the 'fight or flight response' and it's undoubtedly one of the reasons why we are still around to discuss this matter! There is also a 'freeze' response, which can be useful sometimes but is less helpful in the context of hurtling trains!

This emergency response system stood our ancestors in good stead when they had to fight or run away from ferocious animals and it's still potentially very useful to us in our day to day lives when crossing roads, avoiding muggers or dealing with door-to-door salesmen.

The limbic system is very primitive. It does our thinking in black and white, either/or, fight or flight. It's not very logical, but it doesn't have to be logical because that's not what it's for (we have a higher cortex for the logical stuff). It's just there for our survival and it's brilliant in that role.

However, if we spend a lot of time in a hyper-aroused, emotional state, the rational brain may never get much of a look in. Instead, our emotional brain tries to sort things out and, being ill-fitted for that task, it digs itself into an ever-deepening hole. Our emotional secretary and super-vigilant security guards are well placed to get us out of the way of oncoming buses but are less reliable when making decisions about how to spend our money, whether or not have that drink or whether or not to punch that guy in front of us on the nose.

"Emotion unchecked by reason is one of the greatest betrayers of mankind."

Dr. Paul Brunton

Just as in the story, there are times when the system goes into meltdown: the freeze response puts the amygdalae on permanent red-alert until we re-set the pattern-matching to an appropriate level. Fortunately, this model empowers us to do that and there are therapists who are able to help with that process. Using this model, they have enabled many people to lift depression, overcome anxiety, phobias and the after-effects of traumatic events and restore their mental equilibrium very quickly.

Even without a therapist to assist us, when we are feeling calm and our rational brain is in charge, we can sometimes see more clearly which of our habitual thought patterns or circumstances in our lives are causing us hassle, and how to change these in positive ways, rather than worry about them.

Using the APETS model, we may be able to:

A - change the Activating event (our environment and circumstances),

P – change our mental maps: the templates used in the Pattern-matching process (a suitable therapist can help us to do this, using a thing called 'the rewind technique'),

E – lower our Emotional temperature (by having strategies to calm ourselves down),

T – change our Thoughts from unhelpful ones to helpful ones, replacing scary worries with practical solutions. (To do this, it is important to calm down first so that the manager is in charge, rather than the secretary.)

S - When we, as the owner of the brain, can stand back and look at this whole system calmly, we have the power to change our thoughts, change our emotions, choose to amend any faulty mental maps and choose our actions, so if you want to change your life, change your mind or, as my husband says: "change your reality by changing your mentality since what you think about, you bring about."

A Story of Apes and Pets

As Griffin and Tyrell point out, there's a good way of remembering the APET model: When we are over-emotional, the mind is an APE and out of control: when we are calm it becomes A PET and our rational brain is calling the shots.

The owner (the inner Self that observes this whole process) is ultimately in control and doesn't have to put up with any more monkey-business!

We can tell when we are in our emotional brain or 'monkey mind' when we start to engage in catastrophic thinking. If the language we are using in our speech or in our thoughts is very negative and peppered with words like "always", "everything" and "everywhere", this can give us a clue that maybe we need to step back a bit and let our emotions settle down so that our rational brain can gain a wider, and probably more helpful, view of the situation. Not that the rational brain is always wise and helpful, of course. A 'negative attributional style', the habit of always focussing on the bad stuff, can quickly have us back in the hands of the emotional secretary and spiralling into the doldrums. We don't need to be overly positive all the time either. Like yin and yang, it's finding a balance that's important.

This ability to choose what we think, how we feel and what we do is what makes us truly human and is the basis of our freedom.

How to Lift Your Mood

It may come as a bit of a surprise to know that we are not innocent victims of our moods. In fact there's a whole lot we can do to change them. As James Davies suggests in his book *Cracked*, the popular myth that our psychological difficulties are the result of a chemical imbalance in the brain may be another of those back-to-front notions that tend to perpetuate the problem. What if at least some of the perceived chemical imbalances can be triggered by the kind of thoughts going on in our heads? Might there be certain habits that are more or less guaranteed to make us feel better or worse?

Several years ago, an experiment was carried out and was televised as a documentary. Two identical twins were separated for a whole day, during which they were exposed to different environmental conditions. For example, one twin stayed in a hotel room that was bright and cheerful while the other had drab and gloomy decor. The reading materials and music they were exposed to were either inspiring or sad. At the end of the day, the normally happy-go-lucky twins met up in a shopping centre and discovered that their moods had polarised: one felt on top of the world while the other, perhaps predictably, felt very down and despondent.

So no surprises there then, but it may be useful to take a quick look at other subtle influences that can be at play in our daily lives, and how we can shift them in a more helpful direction, if necessary.

If you are feeling fine at the moment, you might like to skip this section. Of course, if you are in a very bad situation, or you are suffering from post-traumatic stress or a serious addiction, the priority is to get appropriate help as soon as possible.

However, if you are just feeling generally down, here are a few practical suggestions that might help you to feel better very quickly.

1. Let the sunshine in. Just taking that first step of opening the curtains could be one of the most powerful things you can do. While many of us have taken to heart the advice to wear sunscreen, or hide in the shade during the summer months, some exposure to the sun each day allows the cells beneath our skin to make Vitamin D, which not only enables our bones to absorb calcium but also helps us to stay mentally alert and less likely to suffer from 'brain fog'. And, while we're on the subject of vitamins, you'll have heard of course that fruit, vegetables, vitamins, minerals and omega 3 oils appear to be good for the brain.

2. Remember to move. We've said a lot about sitting still and meditating but moving around is just as important. You might be inspired to hear that research has found that exercise is as good as anti-depressants for lifting your mood, and without the potentially harmful side-effects. You have probably heard of endorphins, natural pain killers, similar to opium, which are released when we exercise, giving us a sense of well-being.

3. Get some practical help if you need it. Whether this is police protection, the ability to deliver a good pre-emptive strike, financial advice, medical assistance or just a bit of help with the cleaning, we all need a hand sometimes and there is no particular merit in trying to cope with everything on our own.

4. Get clear about what you really want from life. Use the power of your imagination to create a Vibrant Vision of how you would like your world to be.

155

5. Spring-clean your life. Declutter your living environment. Pass stuff on, recycle it, organise what's left. Think Zen. It's amazing how your internal clarity increases with the awareness of organised space around you.

6. Do something meaningful and worthwhile. If you were a hundred and ten and looking back on your life, what would you like to be remembered for? If you haven't done it yet, how soon can you start? Now tends to be a good kind of time.

7. Be careful of any statements that you make about yourself, whether you are thinking them in your head or saying them out loud to other people. These are the self-fulfilling prophecies which end up forming our sense of identity (and other people's impressions of us). Your identity is not something you are stuck with; you create it by choosing any descriptions of yourself rather than leaving them to form by default or by going along with what you think others say about you. While some people may be born into more helpful circumstances than others, resourceful, successful people are not born that way, they choose to be resourceful and successful. Some of them have surmounted considerable challenges and perhaps become stronger and more resourceful because of what they have learned from any setbacks on the way! Make a habit of looking for the best in life and in people (including yourself). What we put our attention on tends to become our reality.

8. Learn to recognise the tricks your emotional brain plays when you're angry, upset, scared or otherwise emotionally aroused. It's called black and white thinking. For example "They are wrong, I am right, and there's no common ground in between". Such thinking is often illogical: "It always happens to me because I'm a Sagittarius" and global: "Everything is terrible!" Get into the habit of eliminating the words "everything", "everywhere" and "always" from your

vocabulary and your rational brain will thank you for it. A passing challenge is not necessarily a catastrophe.

9. Find ways to unwind. Whether it's meditation that helps you to feel peaceful, or Tai Chi, or Qigong, or Yoga, or swimming, or sitting by a stream, or playing football, the important thing is to have few strategies that work for you when you feel the need to chill out and calm down. The calmer your mind, the more easily you can start to see things in a clearer perspective.

10. Phone a friend or ask the audience. You know what they say about a problem shared. It's good to unburden ourselves, and sometimes hearing some fresh thoughts on a subject can help us to get a handle on it. The more we get out and meet new people, the better chance we have of meeting a few who are on our wavelength and will be there for us when we need them. And of course we can also be there for them when they need us. It's amazing how helping other people can make us feel better very quickly by taking our minds off our own concerns for a while.

In general:

Life is an opportunity to be lived, not a problem to be faced.

So you might as well be happy.

Chapter 6 - Choosing What to Think

"The greatest weapon against stress is our ability to choose one thought over another."

William James

We have already seen that rumination – misusing our imagination by going over and over our problems in our heads – is one of the surest routes into the spiral of anxiety and depression, yet many people think they have no choice about what goes on in the mind most of the time. They may envy people who seem to be in control of their thoughts or those who say that they are able to choose not to think about anything at all if they decide not to.

To be able to choose what goes on in your own mind is a valuable skill and it does seem to come more naturally to some people than to others. I know a girl who, at the age of four, used to mentally line up all her current thoughts in the imaginary space in her mind's eye, put the ones that were useful back into her head and then let the others blow away and forget about them.

Such a gift, however, appears to be quite rare. For most people, it's a learned skill that requires practice. The trick is to be patient and not to hit ourselves over the head for 'failing' in some way if we don't always manage to get rid of unwanted thoughts or keep our mind in a state of pristine clarity. It wouldn't be helpful for us to be empty-headed all the time anyway, we just need to find a balance between using our thought processes in a way that enables us to function well in the world and having a bit of down-time to unwind and re-charge our batteries.

One of the saddest things that I have noticed in my life is that the very people who stand to benefit most from the practice of meditation are often those who are the most reluctant to give it a go. People suffering from chronic anxiety will say to me: "I am my thoughts and I don't want anything to do with all that weird stuff like mindfulness and meditation. I did have a go once anyway and I couldn't do it. It's too hard. There was too much going on in my mind."

And of course, they have a point. Even skilled meditators will find thoughts popping up in their minds like bubbles in a glass of champagne or leaves floating past on a stream. That's normal. It's just the way the mind works. However, if we then wade in to inspect the leaves more closely, we are whisked away into places we never intended to go. Most of the time, we are not even aware that we have done this until much later, when we have been led a merry dance around our hopes and fears and memories and brought back to the present moment by some external distraction.

With practice, though, we gradually learn how to avoid paying too much attention to this random surface froth. We don't need to click on the pop-up menus on our mental computer screen, we can just focus on the background and let them fade away, as they often tend to do after a few seconds if we don't click on them. Thoughts don't have any power to sweep us away if we don't give them our attention, they just dissolve back into the depths of the quiet mind.

If we are feeling very anxious at the outset, however, we may need a bit of help to quieten the mind. To be left alone to 'sit with our fear' for hours at a time, on some long retreat, might encourage us to analyse our problems even more and so increase our anxiety.

The same applies to sitting with our anger. We may have been told to look at our thoughts and emotions in a non-judgemental, compassionate way and, indeed, there may be lessons to be learned from the discovery of where our anger is coming from, but to sit for hours inspecting our rage is likely to have a magnifying effect, as is knocking the living daylights out of a punch-bag, or stomping on balloons or, worse still, seeking revenge against an alleged perpetrator! A sense of outrage may be what motivates us to take action against perceived injustice but, even if our perceptions appear to be accurate and our responses seem to be justifiable, allowing that anger to become all-consuming so that it dictates all of our thoughts, words and actions can, potentially, have devastating consequences for people's lives, including our own.

Discovering Peace

When we are very emotionally aroused, what might be more helpful is to spend a few minutes simply watching our breathing, taking a little more time to breathe out than to breathe in, so that we feel more peaceful and at ease. This type of breathing activates the parasympathetic nervous system and induces the 'relaxation response', which is the opposite of the fight-or-flight response and was first described by Dr Herbert Benson from the Harvard Medical School. As well as making us feel more peaceful, as chemicals like serotonin take over from the likes of adrenalin (epinephrine) and cortisol, it allows our rational boss to take over from our emotional secretary and get a more accurate take on the situation.

Once we are feeling calm and we have a bit of time to just sit there, watching the breathing, we might benefit from the presence of a trusted companion who can gently remind us, from time to time, to drop any thoughts that arise as soon as we notice them, and lightly return our attention to the breathing. Or, of course, we can do this on our own. Even five minutes spent practicing this skill can provide some relief from distressing thoughts and have a carry-over effect of helping us to feel more serene and in control as we go about our everyday lives.

Maybe we can develop a habit of stepping back into that calm space and taking a wider view, even when people around us are 'winding us up'. Perhaps this can help us to avoid the black-and-white thinking, or tunnel-vision, of our stress response and allow us the time to consider other viewpoints and find solutions that are acceptable to all. We may even become one of the peacemakers that the world so sorely needs right now.

When people say that they are not 'good at' meditation, what might not be immediately obvious to them, as they beat themselves up for their 'failure', is that they have already achieved considerable success. The fact that they noticed all those thoughts going on in the mind is a good sign. All that remains is to ask "what was it that did the noticing?"

Love and Service

"The more we care for the happiness of others, the greater is our own sense of well-being. Cultivating a close, warm-hearted feeling for others automatically puts the mind at ease. All major religious traditions carry basically the same message, this is love, compassion and forgiveness. The most important thing is they should be part of our daily lives."

The Dalai Lama

Being completely absorbed in our own thoughts and feelings is not the best route to health, happiness or enlightenment. Even meditation, while clearly a valuable skill, can be an entirely self-centred process if it is practiced while we live in isolation. If we wish to gain a fresh and empowering perspective on life, we must acknowledge the fact that we share this world with seven billion other people. The sages therefore recommend that, in addition to practicing meditation, we should put the needs of others first and act for their good.

By focusing our attention on the needs of others, we not only increase our chances of doing something helpful for them but we also reduce the power of our own ego. Paradoxically, by being 'selfless' we come closer to discovering the Self. Most 'spiritual paths', therefore, list love and service as essential components on the journey.

There is little point in attempting to serve others, however, if we do it with reluctance or some thought of gain, whether material or spiritual. Service must be spontaneous and arise naturally, straight from the heart, out of our love for other people and for all other creatures.

Love arises naturally from service, just as service arises naturally from love since, through love, we may experience a genuine concern for the needs of others and feel inspired to help them if we can; therefore unconditional love and service are complementary and both can be seen as inevitable consequences of the enlightened viewpoint which causes us to love our neighbour as our Self and to act accordingly.

"Love is the bridge between you and everything."

Rumi

Insight and Ethics

Through love and service, we may come to glimpse other people as our Self. It is not just empathy - the ability to put oneself into other people's shoes - or even the belief that, underneath, we are all human beings, irrespective of our race, class, gender or culture. It is more than this. It is a fundamental realisation that we are all essentially connected and formed from the same substance, just as a range of pots can be moulded from the same clay.

We begin to see that appearances, opinions, beliefs - everything that gives each person their individuality - are of little importance compared with what we all share, the real Self in all of us, which is essentially the same. At this point, it becomes impossible to hate anyone. Without hate, there is no desire to harm anyone, and a real desire arises to protect others from harm and to work for their good. We may come to judge all our actions by this standard. Through the removal of hate and prejudice, it becomes possible to love everyone. Genuine concern for their physical, mental and spiritual well-being then motivates every action and the course we take in life and service becomes as natural as breathing.

The Importance of Asking Questions

As the Dalai Lama suggests, never say "Yes, yes, yes"; ask "Why? Why? Why?" It doesn't matter how far we have come in terms of our physical, emotional and spiritual development if we are still following on blindly without question. At some stage, we need to begin to ask: just who are we entrusting with the task of knowing what is best for us? Do the people we look up to really have our best interests at heart or is their attention firmly fixed on personal financial profit or power? Until we ask such questions, we are stuck inside the machine with nowhere else to go.

When we ask questions, however, our perception may begin to shift. If we see that our society is not working well for everyone, that our trusted politicians are causing wars in our name, or that they are simply human like the rest of us and often make mistakes; if we see that our trusted sources of information are lying to us or that a substantial number of our neighbours are homeless while our ruling elite live in luxury and avoid paying taxes, we may start to wonder who is really responsible for all of that. Are the people in charge deliberately misusing or neglecting us or are they just fallible human beings who are not up to the daunting tasks we set them, yet we hold them responsible for our happiness?

Who voted them into power anyway? Have we ever decided not to vote and so allowed others to own the election? Have we ever turned a blind eye to the warnings of so-called 'conspiracy theorists' or voted in the light of things we had read about on social media, without checking the facts for ourselves? As we complain about the incompetence of our leaders, might we perhaps admit that we, ourselves, must share some of that responsibility?

In a last-ditch effort to apportion blame elsewhere, might we sometimes even blame the Almighty for our suffering?

Acknowledging our own responsibility can make us feel very uncomfortable but perhaps it is at such times that we begin to gain a more accurate picture of the world we live in and make more informed choices about what to believe and how to behave.

Blame and Responsibility

By responsibility, I am not talking about blame. Blaming ourselves for our misfortunes is just as destructive as blaming other people and/or God. Blame limits us, destroys our self-esteem, blocks our creativity and can soon have us wallowing in self-loathing and depression. Responsibility, on the other hand, inspires us to see problems as challenges and to look for solutions and ways to bring about positive changes for the benefit of everyone. You don't need to be Mahatma Ghandi or Martin Luther King to bring about changes, but these are good examples of people who asked questions, identified the challenges and then took on the responsibility of working out creative solutions and taking peaceful action to bring them about.

In our working lives, we may stop blaming our boss for our low wages and either ask for a pay rise or find out about how to get a different job. If we have no work, we may stop blaming our bad luck and become an entrepreneur, write a book, set up a school, help the homeless or do whatever else we can think of to improve the lives of others.

On a global scale, when we look at the state of the planet, we may feel so overwhelmed by the scale of the challenges ahead of us that we become paralysed into inactivity or disbelief or we look around to find out who is to blame. All of these responses are very human and understandable but less than helpful in our present situation. What may be more useful is for us to ask questions that can lead to a better understanding of the situation. Perhaps we can then find the strength and ingenuity to meet these challenges by recognising our shared responsibility and by working together, cooperatively and supportively, to preserve the natural world and avoid damaging it further. Perhaps the Garden of Eden was not so much a myth as a misinterpretation. Perhaps the whole Earth is our garden and, rather than having dominion over it, we are its caretakers and we are all responsible for its maintenance.

Questioning may begin in childhood but often becomes intense during adolescence, or following a traumatic event, or in times of crisis, or in old age when one is more conscious of the inevitability of death. At such times, we may feel a burning need to find meaning in our lives and try to make sense of it all.

Finding Meaning

Our biggest mental map is our overall world-view which, hopefully, gives our lives a meaningful context. If you are currently struggling to find meaning in your own life right now, you might like to ask yourself the following questions:

If you were one hundred years old and looking back at your life, what would you like your life to have been about?

What meaning do you choose to give to your life right now?

What meaning for the existence of the whole of creation would make sense to you at the very deepest level?

If, in your very old age, you were to recognise your purpose in life and you could go back to this moment, right here and now, as you read these words, what would you choose to do?

Perhaps meaning is not something that is there to be discovered; perhaps it is something that you get to choose. The freedom to choose comes from finding the centre.

Chapter 7 – How To Find The Centre

"We are so engrossed with the objects, or appearances revealed by the light, that we pay no attention to the light. The thing to do is to concentrate on the seer and not on the seen, not on the objects, but on the Light which reveals them."

Ramana Maharshi

This chapter forms the heart of what this book is about: a practical way to look at the world and our place within it. I am by no means the first person to attempt to create such a model. If you google the words manas, buddhi, chitta and ahamkara you will find a plethora of diagrams and explanations that reflect thousands of years of study of how the mind works and how we can discover the 'witness self' at the core of our being. The Hindus, Sufis and many others have studied the workings of the mind in depth over the centuries.

More recently, psychologists and neuroscientists have made considerable progress in finding out how the human brain works. They have generated complex flow diagrams of how we store and retrieve memories in the short term and long term and they have speculated about where, in all of that, we might discover the processes that give rise to our individual conscious and unconscious thoughts and our overall awareness that we exist.

While such models provide an interesting basis for thought, discussion and further investigation and, for some people, may lead to great insights in the long term, they are generally too complex to be accessible to everyone. I believe that what we need right now is something much simpler; something easier to remember and to apply in our everyday lives; something verifiable by our own experience and that doesn't require years of study in a university or ashram to get our heads around; something that can help us, very quickly, to shift our world-view in a positive and constructive manner.

The model I have found most helpful is the sun analogy, in which each of us is like a ray of the same sun, always looking outwards, seeing only its neighbouring rays, which appear to be separate from itself. This model draws together some of the basic ideas from Eastern traditions and Western science and hopefully may help to reconcile the two approaches.

I have based my own version of this model on the APET model and have taken the liberty of extending this to the APETS model, where the S represents the Observing Self. While the APET model looks at how the brain of one human being works, it only addresses one single ray of the sun. Although the Observing Self is also recognised by many as being an essential component of our mental health, it may still be considered to be the Self behind the single ray. In what follows, we will be considering the sun in its entirety: our model relates to the whole of humanity and indeed to the whole of existence.

This is such an empowering model that I have used it many times with groups of students as the basis for an exercise in my philosophy and meditation classes. Some of those students are themselves doctors, teachers and therapists who have then gone on to use it in their own classes or therapy groups, where it has proved to be very beneficial to participants. It would be great if everyone on the planet could have a go at this exercise, as it provides people with a very powerful opportunity to wake up very quickly.

So let's start with what we do and I will explain it as we go along.

"I've been looking for a long, long time,
for this thing called love,

I've ridden comets across the sky,
and I've looked below and above.
Then one day I looked inside myself,
and this is what I found,
A golden sun residing there,
beaming forth God's light and sound."

Rumi

The Walk to the Centre

When I do this exercise with students in my classes, the first thing we need is a large enough space, sufficient for the whole class – anything from about five to twenty people - to form the biggest circle they can while holding hands with arms outstretched. The space could be a room, a hall or a suitable space outdoors.

Next, we imagine that in the centre of the circle there is a sun and each of us is standing on a different ray.

Then we all turn our backs to the sun and look outwards from the edge of the circle and we ask ourselves the question: "What am I?"

The following is an account of what I might say to the group at each stage of the exercise.

The Outermost Edge - The Body

At this outermost level, at the leading edge of our ray, all we can see is what is in front of us. If we see each other at all, our view is limited to those few people nearest to us and none of us can see the sun behind us. When we look at each other, we just see physical bodies and the differences between them, though the idea of difference would not

169

register out here because here, at the very edge, we see ourselves as just a body and nothing else.

Here at the edge, we have senses and reflexes that allow us to interact with our surroundings. We can recoil from things that are too hot or too cold, respond to light and sound and hunger and so forth - but supposing that was all we could do.

Supposing that all there was to me was just this physical body with its basic responses to its environment, like some primitive life form or an android programmed only to react to stimuli in very basic ways. Is that all there is to being human? Clearly it is not. Clearly, as a human being, I am more than just a body.

The body changes all the time, with cells continuously dying off and being replaced. Food molecules are continually being broken down, used and passed back out into the environment. My body, if I can call it "me" at all, is just a temporary holding pattern for the atoms that I have eaten, drunk or breathed in during the last few years. An oxygen atom in the air I just breath in might, during its career, have spent time in the lungs and brains of monarchs and beggars. A carbon atom in my hand right now might once have been part of dinosaur's toenail or a blob of lava in an exploding volcano and all the atoms in my body and yours were born in the heart of suns!

Those atoms that were present in my body when I was born have been scattered to the far-flung corners of the world and are now a part of skies, oceans, soil, plants, animals and other people. Moreover, atoms, as we have seen, are simply vibrating patterns of energy within the vast field of energy underlying everything. So, miraculous as it may be, this body is not all there is to me. Whatever it is that I am, there must be a bit more to me than that.

So what else am I? Well for one thing, I have access to an on-board computer, which I call a brain, that processes all of this incoming information.

At this point we all take a small step backwards towards the centre of the circle.

The First Step Back: Pattern-matching

So far, all we have been aware of is information coming from our senses. When we studied the APET model in the previous chapter, we saw that when the brain receives input from the senses, the information is processed through the amygdalae. A pattern-matching process takes place via the set of maps or templates through which we scan the world. We compare things and label them with names and preconceptions of what they are like and what they might mean. The new information then gets an emotional tag as the amygdalae send it deeper into the limbic system for further analysis. So we now take a second step back towards the centre.

The Second Step Back - Emotions

So that's something that sets me a bit apart from a primitive life-form or an android already - I have emotions. I not only see, hear, touch, taste and smell the world around me, I have feelings about it as well.

This is useful for my survival: it gives me fight or flight capabilities. It allows me to feel attracted to some things and helps me to avoid some of the unpleasant stuff out there. However, my emotions tend to change from hour to hour, even moment to moment, especially if I hear that something awful has happened, or if I get a bit of unexpected good news. Being so changeable in nature, clearly my emotions are not me, which is just as well really because sometimes these feelings can be very strong and not particularly useful if I get too bogged down in them. If I get really worked up, I tend to get stuck here and my

171

primitive limbic system has to try to do all my thinking for me, however illogical and unhelpful its efforts might be. What to do?

We step back further.

Third Step Back - Rational Thoughts

Fortunately, if I can calm myself down sufficiently, I can step back deeper into myself and access my rational, thinking brain or higher cortex, which can even choose to over- ride emotions if it wants to.

I have access to memories that help me to make sense of things, within the context of time and space, and enable me to learn from my experiences. I have the ability to name and categorise everything I experience, which allows me to communicate with other people around me using language. I have an imagination which allows me to create pictures, compose music, express my feelings through dance or write poetry. I can calculate, analyse and plan and, in my mind's eye, I can visualise anything, from the entire known universe to the sub-atomic world.

However, I can get stuck in all this mental clutter sometimes and I can have difficulty switching it off, especially at night when I want to go to sleep. Happily, I can also learn techniques to help me to do that. I can meditate and step back to a quiet place beyond thought where I am able to rest without disturbance from the mind and its mischief.

Perhaps an android could be programmed to do most of these things too. It could store and retrieve vast amounts of information and calculate complicated sums beyond anything my brain could cope with. But could an android have imagination? Could an android have its own motives, rather than those of its programmer? Could an android have original thought and free-will?

I'm a human being. Isn't that a bit more than a collection of parts that can process information and be programmed to do certain things? In any case, my thoughts are continually changing and therefore there must be more to me than my thoughts. Maybe there is more to me than even my most cherished opinions and beliefs, considering that these are very different to the ones I used to cherish during my childhood or my teenage years. Time to step back a bit.

The Fourth Step Back - Intuition

Stepping back into myself a bit more, to the part of me that watches the content of my thoughts. I can see that I am thinking.

I can observe my thoughts as they come and go. I can choose what I think about, I can choose not to think at all and I can choose to think about nothing.

Since thoughts, opinions, beliefs and feelings are always changing and since I can stand back and observe these changes, I am clearly not those thoughts, opinions, beliefs and feelings. When I watch these movements of the mind, surely I am whatever it is that is doing this watching.

There's something rather interesting about this level. If I am trying to work out a particularly complicated problem, there are times when I can just switch off all the mental churning around and go for a swim, or a walk around the block, or have a nap, and then suddenly the solution to the problem emerges, seemingly out of nowhere, not from my logical brain but from some deeper part of me which I call my intuition.

We have not yet programmed robots to have emotions; could we give them intuition? Or will that always be a defining characteristic of humanity that sets us apart from our mechanical creations? Who knows? But even if we did manage to create some super-android that could do all these things, is there still something more to a human being than a machine with feelings, thoughts or even intuition?

Perhaps the key to answering this one lies in the words "human being". I am a human being, not a human doing. Robots are programmed to do things. Even if they ever became so sophisticated that they could reproduce themselves and programme each other, so they didn't need us any more, would they also have an awareness of being, like Isaac Asimov's *I Robot*?

We step back again.

The Fifth Step Back - "I Am Something" and "I Am All."

Is there not something behind all the mechanisms of my mind which is deeper and more fundamental than all the layers we have discussed so far, a sense of "I am something"? When all the labels I place on myself are gone, when I take off all the hats I wear on a day to day basis such as "I am a mother", "I am a friend" or even, "I am human", is there not still that sense of "I am something", albeit a nameless something?

At this point, our circle has shrunk to the point where there is no longer any space between us. We are pressed shoulder to shoulder and we are able to hold hands and become aware that "I am All".

At this point we all turn around to face the centre of the circle.

The Centre

Now that we are finally facing each other, we realise that, if we all took one more step, we would be standing on the exact same spot and that is: "I AM".

This is the state that we can achieve during meditation, when there are no thoughts, nothing to disturb the perfect peace and pure awareness of being, without being any particular thing. It is not spectacular. It is so ordinary, in fact, that we can overlook it for a lifetime, yet there is nothing more profound.

"The heart is nothing but the sea of Light."

Rumi

I wonder if a robot would have this "I am" sense: a switched-on, aware but not yet thinking or doing anything kind of awareness; a ready state without any kind of content or function - just being and, most importantly, being aware of that being. I know that I am aware that I AM.

I also know that people around me appear to work in much the same way. They have thoughts and feelings and flashes of inspiration and intuition, and when they are able to calm down and allow their minds to be still, they can all be simply aware of "I AM". And that's' the interesting point here. Maybe that "I AM" in them is the same as the "I AM" in me.

Standing here at the centre of the circle, with all our differences left behind at the outside edge, I can know that this "I AM" is the same in me, in you and in everything. All of us can know this, right now.

I've just described my view of the world from the outside in, like a line from my surroundings via my body, feelings and thoughts to the innermost part of myself, the "I AM" that is my deepest - and perhaps my only real - Self.

There are some who would say that the deepest part of me is my Ego, my collection of memories, experiences, desires, opinions, beliefs and idiosyncrasies. Yet, as we have just seen, all of those ideas are peripheral and ever-changing.

Deep inside of me there is something that never changes, something which quietly watches all of my thinking and feeling and ideas and imagined vulnerabilities, without being affected by any of it.

Each person may spend some or all of a lifetime imagining himself or herself to be a separate body, confined by skin and containing a specific set of feelings, memories, thoughts, opinions and beliefs which they cherish as their own identity and will go to almost any lengths to protect. From this limited viewpoint, other people are seen as separate from, and different to, our self and this is the cause of most of the suffering in this world. This individual, separate self, or ego, may even imagine that it's true inner self is a frightened child who needs to be nurtured and supported by others. Nothing could be further from the truth!

Were we to look back once in a while, we would see that all the rays arise continually from the same source and that no thing and no one is separate from that source, nor has it ever been separate, nor will it ever be separate. There is only the One. Rather than discovering ourselves to be weak or vulnerable, we would be stunned by our own magnificence.

"You realize that, all along, there was something tremendous within you, and you did not know it."

Paramahansa Yogananda

Individuals may overlook it, avoid looking at it, refuse to believe it - just as a wave may choose not to believe in the existence of the ocean upon the surface of which it forms and subsides - but believing it is there is not required, the ocean continues to wave, whatever the wave thinks it is, and the rays of the sun may argue among themselves if that is their choice; meanwhile the sun simply continues to shine.

"All religions, all this singing, one song.
The differences are just illusion and vanity.

The sun's light looks a little different on this wall than it does on that wall, and a lot different on this other one, but it's still one Light."

Rumi

Part 3 - The View From the Centre

Awakenings

The world is in a sorry state

Because we all feel separate.

The thought that I exist within

A boundary I call my skin

And everything and everywhere

Is outside "me" and all "out there"

Is what allows a man to take

All that he can, for his own sake

While others starve and children die

And ice caps melt and rivers dry.

Yet quantum physicists agree

That there's a whole lot more to me

Than flesh and blood and bone and brain,

This little blob of joys and pain.

There is in fact another view

Of what is me and what is you:

Each atom of what I call me

Is nothing more than energy –

A ripple within time and space -

And every atom of your face

Is made from the same stuff as mine -

Vibrations within space and time -

As is the earth beneath our feet
And every person we may meet
And every stone and every flea
And every leaf on every tree
And every tear we'll ever cry
And every star within the sky.
Like overlapping notes of sound
We dance among the cosmic ground;
One Ground, One Song, One Dance, One Sea
And I am you and you are me.
I know you know that this is true
For you are me and I am you.

Chapter 8 - Empowerment

The sun analogy is an extremely empowering model through which to view the world. As single rays of that same sun, if we can make a habit of stepping back and taking a wider view, we can stop seeing ourselves as a body or as a set of thoughts, opinions or beliefs that we have collected over the years: that's just our ego, which is as insubstantial as the wind. Instead we can step right back to the centre and look out along our ray from a universal standpoint.

Interestingly, in some parts of India, an old system is still practiced, whereby each child is informed of their cosmic identity before their education begins. They still love their parents and value their own uniqueness but they do not see themselves as a limited individual.

"Education is empowerment. You should never empower a limited identity. If you empower a limited identity, violence is a natural consequence of that."

Sadhguru Jaggi Vasudev

Imagine the world as it might be if, instead of seven billion individual identities fighting each other to protect their rights to exist, there were seven billion people who were able to value and respect the rights of every individual while also recognising their universal identity and knowing that we are all, essentially, one.

Liberty and Freedom

It is when we step back to the centre and realise that the sun is our true identity that we gain the power of choice. We can see our connection with everything, our unity, and we can see that our mind and body are instruments that we can use. We can use our mind constructively to think what we choose to think, feel what we choose to feel, act as we choose to act and, to a large extent, be what we choose to be, which gives us true freedom, even when we do not have the liberty to go where we wish to go.

Living out at the edge of the circle causes us so many problems because we become entirely focussed on superficial differences, which we tend to take far too seriously. It is this view that leads to the endless suffering that we create for ourselves. On a personal level, it can lead to dissatisfaction with ourselves and our neighbours. Taken to the extreme, it is at the root of what many religions would call our 'sins'.

Is There Such a Thing As Sin?

Interestingly, the word "sin" is an archery term which means 'missing the mark'.

If we imagine looking down on our circle from above, with each step backwards forming a new ring, it kind of looks like a target. In the outer circles, the passionate rays (the little ego-selves), under the illusion that they are separate and different from their neighbours, are the source of all 'sin'. It is out here at the edge that we see other people as 'different' and so can feel jealousy, hatred and all the other thoughts and emotions that allow us to treat each other badly. It's where our possessiveness and our desire for ownership and revenge come from and it lies at the heart of our warmongering.

The view from the centre, on the other hand, is quite the opposite. It is the most empowering way to see the world, both as individuals and as a species and it is the source of our compassion.

We have long been advised that the antidote to our sins is atonement.

181

Atonement as At-one-ment

At the centre of the 'target' there is only the "I AM": the Self of all. When we see that we are all one, there can be no sin because all greed, fear, anger, jealousy, desire and hostility - all the thoughts and emotions which cause us to harm ourselves and each other - are associated with the outer layers, where we see only the differences and imagine ourselves to be separate.

What lies at the heart of me is what lies at the heart of you, at the heart of everyone else on the planet, at the heart of all life and at the heart of reality itself. There is no vulnerable 'inner child'. We are one with everything.

The process of re-discovering the centre is therefore called at-one-ment. To overcome 'sin' – our erroneous view of each other as separate - we must atone. We must shift our world-view and see that we are all one.

Re-membering

When we are right out at the edge, we can't see the sun behind us, we only see what it illuminates in front of us, and everything we see, everything that seems to be 'out there', is an expression of the same sun that is the source of our own being.

When they hear this for the first time, people often have the feeling that they already knew this, like a memory that they had somehow forgotten. Now they remember, or re-member.

Suppose you worked in the catering industry and you were set the task of slicing vegetables with a sharp knife. Sadly, you manage to cut off one of your fingers in the process. Fortunately, however, a quick thinking colleague elevates your arm and puts pressure on the wound while another takes your finger, pops it into a plastic bag and wraps it

182

in a tea towel, then puts that into a bag full of ice. They then get you off to the hospital where, thanks to their timely assistance and the miracles of modern surgery, your finger is stitched back on again and, after a couple of months of healing, it is back to being fully functional. That finger would have re-membered.

Finding Your Way Back

From reading this book so far, you will have realised that the way back to the centre is through knowledge, meditation, love and service.

Meditation is like the express train that can take us straight to the centre – to the very core and source of our being. It is the means by which the outer layers of mind are tamed and settled so that we can remember what we are and simply be it. Once we know this, from our own direct experience, we are forever free to step back to the centre at any time and, as we go about our lives in this world at the leading edge of the sunlight, our interactions with our fellow rays tend to be based on love.

Once we have seen and experienced this view for ourselves, we can continue to view the world from the edge, or we can choose to step back and view the world from the centre - the "I AM". This freedom to switch our perspective from the individual to the universal at will is what is known as 'enlightenment'. From that moment onwards, even when we seem to be caught up in the turmoil of our daily lives, we cannot 'unknow' our true identity. It is there at the heart of us all the time, which gives us a steadiness: a deep sense of contentment, even as we continue to face life's endless challenges.

Looking at this picture, how can any of us be separate? And, if there is a God or some kind of cosmic consciousness, how could that be separate from us?

"Jesus said, 'It is I who am the light which is above them all. It is I who am the All. From me did the All come forth, and unto me did the All extend. Split a piece of wood, and I am there. Lift up a stone, and you will find me there.'"

The Gospel of Thomas, Verse 77

Chapter 9 – Taking Control of the Ray

The difference between liberty and freedom can now be seen very clearly. We have liberty when we are free to go where we choose, without restriction: Freedom, on the other hand, is the ability to decide how we look at the world. We can choose to see the bars on the window or the stars beyond them, we can choose to focus on the sunset or the barbed-wire fence, and we can choose the content of our own mind. Knowing our true identity, we get to choose our individual identity and our work in this world and we can, at will, choose to switch our viewpoint from the individual to the universal.

The sun model is, therefore, extremely empowering. With the sun analogy in mind, we not only discover a place that we can go to be free from our thoughts and see everything more clearly, we can also make the return journey, out along our ray, and we are free to make choices every step of the way.

We can choose what to think and so influence the emotions that arise from those thoughts; we can choose our actions and we can even challenge our most deeply held prejudices and fears. We might not be able to do much to change the physical appearance of our bodies, but when it comes to our view of the world and the part we play in it, we have the power to be whatever we choose to be. There can be few thoughts more empowering than that.

Processes In-formation

All of this probably sounds too easy. Can we really choose to change the mental maps that have been ingrained into us by our life experiences and conditioning, or change the habitual thoughts that affect our emotions? Well yes we can. Nothing is fixed. Nothing is broken. We are processes in-formation. To change the way we look at our world and respond to it, we need the correct information. Then we need to practice and develop new and more helpful habits.

As a simple example, if we are given the information that a high fat diet is what causes people to become overweight, and we live according to this belief without being aware of the need for some fats in our diet and the role that refined carbohydrates play in the process of fat storage by over-producing insulin, which prevents us from accessing the energy stored in our fat cells, we may find that our bodies develop in ways that we had not intended. When we are finally provided with the correct information, we are empowered to change our behaviour accordingly and start to re-form in a way that we prefer.

Our process of becoming is more than physical. If we are provided, from birth, with misinformation about our world and our place within it, we can find that everything we believe ourselves to be has been constructed on shaky foundations and these have been influencing our habits, our character and the way we have been living our lives.

When we are armed with the correct information, we can consciously choose what to be, and start to be it. The resulting shift in perception of what we are tends to take care of most of our least helpful thoughts and feelings as well.

On a practical level, you may well ask, how can we possibly 'be what we choose to be'? The first step is to listen to the way we talk about ourselves inside our own heads.

Years ago, I discovered that I had a habit of saying to myself: "I give up!" when life got really difficult. From then on, whenever I caught myself doing that, I immediately switched to something more positive such as: "I can do this!" or "Best foot forward." It worked for me and got me out of the door on the days when I dreaded what was in store for me that day, which was not usually as bad as I thought it was going to be, once I got stuck in.

186

The trick is to catch yourself doing it: that's the point where you have the power to change it. This applies, especially, to any sentence beginning with the words: "I am…"

"I am…" Statements

How many times do you find yourself thinking, or even saying aloud, statements such as "I am hopeless" or "I am useless" or "I am stupid"?

Many of us go through life telling ourselves stories like this every day, often without any idea of where we got these ideas from in the first place.

There's a story I used to tell myself - that I was rubbish at maths - and I know exactly where it came from: a teacher who put me into a lower set for maths on the first day he met me. I had always enjoyed maths up to that point, but that was before I discovered that, according to him, I was useless at it. This belief then shaped not only the expectations of my teachers but also my actual performance in practically every subject I studied throughout the rest of my time in school. From having been a high flyer, I saw myself as being at the bottom of any class, struggling to catch up with all the clever kids.

It was not until I left school that this view of myself changed. At a time when I needed to find employment and the only job available was in a laboratory, I had to agree to go to college on day-release from work and study maths, physics and chemistry at an advanced level. I had always wanted to study physics, so I decided to have a go. Somehow, in spite of my belief that I would not be able to cope with the maths, I not only survived the two years in College but actually thrived on it. I came away with high grades in all subjects, including a distinction in maths, and went on to gain an honours degree in biochemistry and several post graduate qualifications.

What this proved to me is that you can do pretty much anything if you put your mind to it and just give yourself a chance, and there is nothing more powerful in shaping your life than the 'I am' statements you use in your own mind.

Don't let anyone tell you that you are hopeless, useless, stupid or rubbish. What do they know anyway? Most of them will not even remember saying it years later, after they have succeeded in screwing up your life. Especially, never use such terms when you speak to your children or when you talk about yourself.

Any words that follow "I am…" in a sentence become a kind of self-fulfilling prophecy. If you go through life telling yourself that you are unpopular, you will expect other people to avoid you and so behave in ways that come across as either overly 'clingy' or 'stand-offish' to other people, who then avoid you…and so it goes on.

Instead, think of what, in an ideal world, you would choose to be, in terms of your character and personality. Obviously if you are wanting to be ten inches taller or shorter, your "I am" statements are not going to make a lot of difference but when it comes to your mental and psychological outlook, even the simplest shift in your take on things can be transformative.

If you want to change your life, change your mind. Start by mentally stepping back towards the centre and changing any unhelpful "I am" statements. Whenever you notice any negative ones on the tip of your tongue, replace them with something more helpful. Your thoughts, feelings, actions and the way the world responds to you will then rearrange themselves around that.

And of course, when you step right back into the centre, and you know what you really are, your world-view is centred around "I AM" and there is nothing else to add.

*"The universe is not outside of you. Look inside yourself;
everything that you want, you already are."*

Rumi

The Real Power of Prayer

There are two main reasons for praying to an all-powerful, divine being.

1. To give thanks for something.

2. To ask for something, for yourself or others.

Giving thanks for things is good. It means that you have an attitude of gratitude, which is a very healthy way to focus your attention. You are more likely to feel happy and content in this life, even when it throws manure at you, if you are still glad to be alive and thankful for the things you have and for what has gone well for you.

Asking for help for other people is also good because it means that you care about others and are not too tied up in your own misery to notice theirs. It probably means that you are a loving person, inspired by compassion and kindness, and you are sensing your connection and unity with others, even if it is only one other person and does not yet include the whole of mankind or all living creatures.

Asking for something for yourself is not a bad thing. It does not mean that you are selfish or greedy, it most likely means that you have a need that has not been met, and that unfulfilled need is making you unhappy. You might pray every night for more peace, more love, more strength, more courage or whatever and it may seem that nobody is listening to, let alone answering, your prayers. And yet the answer you seek is in the prayer you ask.

189

The Power of Amen

In one language at least, the word 'amen' is used at the end of every prayer. This word, literally, means: "So be it".

For decades of my life, I used to trot out this word according to the instructions given to me as a child, without thinking about why it was there. To me, it was just a customary end-word, a sign of respect to the Almighty perhaps, or just a kind of note that the prayer had now come to an end, like writing 'yours faithfully' and signing your name at the end of a letter. A formality. Even when I heard that it meant 'so be it', that suggested: "so that's all I want to say then, over to you now and whatever happens, let it be so and I will accept it."

It was only much later that I realised that Amen was actually the answer to the prayer.

Suppose you asked someone for more success in your life, and their answer was, "Fair enough. So…be successful then."

In the same way, if you are praying for more love, the answer is: "So, be it!" Be love, be kindness, be healing, be peace, be brave, be whatever it is that you are asking for. This is another paradigm shift that can be transformative. When you have stood at the centre of the circle, realised your true identity and then looked out along your ray and taken ownership of it, you can see how this works.

That ray is the instrument through which you do your work in this lifetime. When you see it for what it is, you can shake off all its limiting beliefs. You don't need them. You are so much more than you give yourself credit for. When you begin to behave as if you are the very embodiment of those qualities you thought you lacked, others will see them in you too. You will then help others the most by simply being yourself.

When you are love, people will sense that love in you and, because it is now what you are, you can give it freely, and the more of it you give, the more it flows back to you.

More even than this, when you are standing at the centre, you don't have to pretend to be love, or to accept it intellectually. You don't have to be a ray pretending to be bright and using that imagined brightness to hide the darkness it imagines to be within itself. The ray is a glorious expression of the light of the sun that you already are. Love, peace, the very essence that your soul has yearned for, is already within you. Love is your own true nature; it is only the limiting beliefs of the ego that cast distortions and clouds to obscure its brightness. When that veil falls away, you just be what you already are and the whole world can bathe in the warmth and light of your love.

Thine is the kingdom, and the power and the glory, because that is what you already are. For ever and ever. So be it.

That is the real power of prayer.

"There is no need to follow that star. It is already within you.
It is that which lights your way and lights your smile."

Zoya

The Inward Journey

How, then, do we recognise the difference between the kind of thoughts that occur out at the edge and those that occur when we are 'centred' and in control of the ray?

Firstly, we know that we are out at the edge when most of our "I am..." statements are negative ones, especially when we are very emotionally upset and our limbic system is doing our thinking, which we can recognise by the black-and-white, all-or-nothing, fight or flight nature of such thoughts and by our tendency to catastrophize everything. As we have already seen, we tend to generalise statements to include words like "always", "everywhere" and "everything" so that all the bad stuff we are experiencing seems permanent and all-pervasive and personal. This can give rise to the impression that: "I am caught up in this world, overwhelmed, out of my depth, separate from everyone and everything. I am a muddle of thoughts and confusion. I am in the grip of strong emotions that I can't control. I am helpless and hopeless."

But hang on. What if we just sit still and replace all of that with:

I am not this body.

I am not these thoughts.

I am not these feelings.

I am aware of something higher.

I am calm, still, waiting.

I am connected to everything.

I am all.

I am.

Now we are at the centre and we can rest here a while. We can heal. We can look again at the ray from the inside out and we can choose the "I am…" statements we use as we take control of the instrument.

The Outward Journey

"I am.

I am all.

I am free.

I am unlimited.

I am loving, brave and kind.

I am creative and strong.

I am working perfectly through this instrument."

Ironically, while we feel powerful and do not lack self-esteem, we are also very humble because we no longer see ourselves as better or worse than any other person or creature. This is the very heart of equality. Whatever we do, we do it for mankind and for all of life on the planet we live on.

This is how we go about creating Heaven on Earth.

Beyond the Fear of Dying

I mentioned earlier that the view of the world I have described in this book overcame my fear of dying yet, as Omar Khyyam famously said: "...of the myriad who before us passed the door of darkness through, not one returned to tell us of the road which, to discover, we must travel too". What possible grounds might I have for offering you reassurance about your own mortality?

Near-death experiences aside - since the jury is still out on the authenticity of these - some of the events I have witnessed in this lifetime do appear to defy any attempts to explain them by science alone. The following is an example which I hope may bring you some comfort.

I was present at the hospital when my dear aunt passed away after a long fight with cancer. The previous day, she had asked me to place my hand on the top of her head to bring her some comfort. After the nurse told me she had 'gone', I again placed my hand on the top of her head, in case she could still feel anything and might find this comforting.

As my hand approached her head, I felt a kind of intense warmth moving at speed through my hand, in through the palm and out through the back. It was not simply that her head was warm to the touch (which it was, though the rest of her body was cold) it was a stream of warmth passing through my hand. I immediately withdrew the hand in astonishment. I felt as if I was somehow invading her privacy during a unique and deeply personal experience.

I have since learned that, in some cultures, there is a belief that the soul leaves the body through the top of the head. Had I known this at the time, I might have dismissed my experience as a psychosomatic event triggered by my own unconscious expectations, but as it was so entirely unexpected, I remain convinced that this was a real phenomenon and it has substantially altered my perceptions of reality and of life and death. It is a perception that I would like to share with others in view of the comfort it can bring to anyone who has lost someone dear to them.

I do not follow any religion, as you may have gathered, and I have always been very sceptical when it comes to 'mysterious energies' and similar other-worldly stuff, yet I knew, with a certainty greater than anything that could have been conveyed to me by books, teachers, priests or others, that my loved one no longer required the use of her physical body and had simply left it behind like an old set of clothes and moved on. This perception can remove any personal fear of dying, which is why I am sharing it with you.

While I am not advocating that we all go off and do lots of research into the realms of the 'paranormal', I do think it is worth considering the possibility that the death of the body is not the end of existence. In life, we are able, through meditation, to switch the attention from the individual to the universal. My personal belief is that the attention simply returns fully to the universal when the pattern of energy we call the body dissolves back into the biosphere. That particular ray may have retreated back into the sun but the sun continues to shine.

"Continually emerging, it returns again and again to nothingness...

To return to the Source is to know perfect peace. I call this a return to life...

If you are like the Tao, you will have eternal life, and you needn't be afraid of dying."

Lao Tzu, in 'The Little Book of the Tao Te Ching', translated by John R. Mabry

The Guru Inside

"Why seek inner peace through sources outside of oneself? Calm the mind and listen to the Source within... Hear what speaks truth to your heart and embrace it completely."

L. Ryokan

Do you need an external guru to help you to find yourself? Maybe, for some, there is much to be gained from travelling to distant countries and spending months or years in ashrams, retreats and monasteries. Maybe it's good to escape from the hectic pace of modern life or the chaos, fear and misery of war-torn nations and just sweep floors, make soup and sit in the lotus position day after day.

Maybe some wise person or other can, through their words and quiet example, remind you of the quietness deep within your own being. All of that is fine, if that's what you feel you need right now.

The point is that the thing you are looking for, and that such wise people may help to reveal to you, is not out there to be looked for. All anyone can ever offer you are clues to remind you of what you already are. Now. This moment. Right here.

There have been people in this world who were considered to possess genius: great writers, musicians, painters and others who had a certain degree of modesty when it came to attributing their works to themselves. Many have said they felt as if a higher power was working through them. Hugh Walpole, in a book called Fortitude, described a writer's task as "listening for the voice of God". Nealle Donald Walsch wrote a whole series of books about conversations with God. Does that mean that all these people were supremely religious or even delusional? Or does it mean that they discovered, and were able to tap into, a deep resource of inspiration and creativity that is within us all, yet most of us remain unaware of?

The scientist Kekule, while racking his brains to work out the structure of benzene, apparently went to sleep and had a dream. Most accounts of his anecdote say that he dreamed of a snake swallowing its own tail, while others say it was a group of monkeys holding hands and dancing in a circle. Whatever, he went on to publish a paper describing the structure of benzene as a hexagonal 'ring' of carbon atoms, the key insight of organic chemistry.

As we have seen when we 'walked to the centre', when our emotions settle and we let go of our attempts to work everything out, we can allow our intuition to provide us with the answers we are looking for. When Nealle Donald Walsh, in the depths of despair, wrote down his questions and the answers that came to him, does it matter if that was really God providing the answers or if it was a deeper part of Walsh's own mind? Maybe the act of writing, which is thought to be an activity associated with the left hemisphere and logical reasoning, calmed down the emotional limbic system long enough for greater clarity of thought to take place and this, combined with access to the creativity of the right hemisphere, allowed intuitive solutions to arise. Whatever the mechanism, the answers were fascinating and made a lot of sense. Those insights took his books to the top of the best seller lists and transformed his life.

It can work for us too. Just find a quiet moment and write down the most burning questions in your mind. If the almighty were to suddenly appear before you, what is it that you would most like to ask? Then write down the answer that comes to mind. Maybe you will see this as God answering your question. Maybe you will see that, on a deep level, you already knew the answer but you were blocking it with your fears, doubts and attempts to fathom it out through logic and reason. Maybe just calming your mind will unblock the access to your rational prefrontal cortex, or maybe your intellect will just take a time out and let your intuition get a look in. Or maybe your God Spot will connect up to the universal awareness that allows you to access more wisdom than you ever knew you possessed. Maybe this is the way that the universal Self is able to express itself most clearly through the individual.

Maybe you will come away with a few words that are transformative. Maybe you will write a book, or a poem, or compose a symphony. When you get out of your own way like this, the results can sometimes be astonishing. When you perform your work in this way, you can enter the state that is popularly known as 'flow'.

"Do not follow the ideas of others, but learn to listen to the voice within yourself. Your body and mind will become clear and you will realize the unity of all things."

Dogen

Flow

You may have had moments when everything just went really well: when you scored that goal, or played that piano, or performed that operation or whatever it was and the whole thing seemed kind of effortless, almost as if it wasn't you doing it but something working through you. This is a natural state that can occur when you let go of your anxieties, overcome any procrastination, ignore any tempting distractions, and just get on with the task in hand and do it for its own sake, in the moment. No 'what if...?'s, no expectations of failure, success or reward. Just that one task, in that moment, with all your attention and a quiet mind, and the task may appear to do itself as you look on in wonder. When your body is no longer the tool of your ego but the instrument through which your true Self works in this world, flow tends to arise, just as, when clouds blow away, the sun shines through without any effort at all.

Chapter 10 - Non-Attachment: A Conversation

Attachment

What is attachment?

Attachment is needing something so much that we convince ourselves that we cannot live without it. The need comes from the desire for the pleasurable attributes of the thing we are attached to, or the fear that we won't be able to manage without it.

What kinds of things do we become attached to?

People. Possessions. Opinions. Beliefs. Experiences.

In what ways does attachment hinder us in our quest for "enlightenment"?

Apart from the pain and distress it may cause to ourselves and to other people, when we are attached we become so focussed on the things we are attached to that we miss the bigger picture.

How is it overcome?

By realising the impermanence of everything and by seeing the universe as it is. This is the paradox. By removing attachment, you see the view, and once you see the view you are no longer attached. Even where it was the briefest glimpse, we can keep bringing it to mind whenever we notice ourselves becoming too attached, until the view we have glimpsed becomes a continuous insight into reality.

What about your family, close friends and loved ones; shouldn't you be attached to them?

No. You love them, cherish them, nurture, support and guide them but leave them free to be themselves. You don't possess them and they don't possess you, and your happiness does not depend on their affection. Loving doesn't imply ownership or dependence.

Detachment

Is non-attachment the same thing as detachment?

No.

What is detachment?

Detachment is mentally and emotionally 'stepping back' from people and things to the point where they are unable to affect you emotionally. Total detachment means cutting yourself off from everyone and everything so that you feel isolated and alone.

What happens if we detach ourselves from everything?

You may feel that you have become an uncaring observer of everything that is going on around you. You can even become completely detached from your will to live and yet remain alive because you lack the will to die. This is a horrible feeling, a bit like coming back into the world as a ghost and unable to connect with, or care about, anyone. In fact this sorry state is a classic symptom of depression.

But isn't that a description of enlightenment: seeing the illusion for what it is and not becoming caught up in it?

No. It's quite the opposite. Detachment is based on the idea that each of us is separate from the rest of the universe. It is this idea which causes so many of our problems (including depression) and leads us to believe that we can possess things or allow ourselves to be possessed or controlled by others. If there is any idea that is guaranteed to prevent us from becoming enlightened, this is it!

Non-attachment

So what is non-attachment?

Non-attachment just means avoiding getting attached to anyone or anything to the point where it obscures your view and your judgement.

If you don't become attached, doesn't that mean you are cut off?

No. You can be connected, without being attached.

What is connection?

Connection is feeling that everyone and everything is your own self. You have reverence and respect for all life. There is no separation, therefore there is no possibility of isolation or loneliness, or of possession or attachment. You don't possess your heart, it's just part of you. So is every living creature on the planet and every star in the sky.

What is it that connects you to others?

You don't need to become connected since you are not separate, you never will be separate and you were never separate to begin with.

But, even if we can accept that knowledge intellectually, what is it that frees us from attachment and allows us to experience that unity or 'connectedness' directly?

Love.

Sidetracks

Once you have this insight and a sense of connection or unity, are there still dangers to be avoided?

When you are fully aware of your unity with everything, there is no attachment, but until that happens, you can still become attached in subtle ways:

* You can become attached to 'spirituality' as a concept.

* You can become overly attached to people who share your 'spiritual awareness', because of the pleasure this gives you.

* You can become attached to your own beliefs and opinions about the path to enlightenment, to the point where you do not consider anyone else's point of view. (This is arrogance.)

* You can be attached to the idea of converting everyone to your beliefs in the hope that it will transform the world and prevent suffering. (This doesn't mean that you shouldn't try to prevent suffering, just that you might be wise to avoid getting overly attached to the idea.).

* You can become attached to meditative states. Meditation is a fine instrument but it's important not to overdo it and to make sure we keep our feet firmly on the ground. As Jack Kornfield said, in his famous book title: *After the Ecstasy; the Laundry*.

With so many traps for the unwary, perhaps it's not surprising that so many cults spring up all over the place, some of them perhaps accidentally, and so many earnest seekers go astray.

How can you avoid arrogance when you have seen the truth?

By remembering that you have only seen the 'truth' as you perceive it from your present position and level of experience. Remember how far you have come and how convinced you once were that what you saw then was the truth, though your perspective may well have shifted since then. It could happen again. Retain humility in everything, particularly when helping others to see what you see. Allow people to make up their own minds and be their own masters. Don't claim to know everything. Don't make them dependent on you. (This is how cults start!) And never dismiss what they say and so miss the wisdom in their words. In the end, arrogance is only possible when there is still some illusion of separation. How can you be arrogant when there is nobody else in the room?

What is the difference between a student and a master?

Ultimately, there is no such thing as a master. We are all students engaged in the fascinating process of attempting to make sense of it all. What we perceive to be masters are those who have made a little more progress than most on the journey and can pause to lend a hand to those behind them and help them to avoid a few pitfalls. The only honest way to teach is to work diligently on our own understanding and our own character. We can be available, honest and open enough to share any insights we may have with those who ask; help them to recognise their own strengths and virtues and live our lives in a way that causes no harm to anyone. Hypocrisy is worse than ignorance. Above all, don't let the idea that people call you a master inflate your ego.

What is the ego?

It is attachment to our own ideas about our individual, little self as a separate entity from everyone else, particularly ideas which cause us to compare ourselves with others or to overestimate or underestimate our own importance.

How can I remove my ego?

You don't need to remove or destroy the ego, only see it for what it is. Seeing everything as yourself puts the little you into clearer perspective. The little you becomes humble because it realises its smallness, yet at the same time it does not find this distressing because it also recognises its interconnectedness with everything and its right to exist, because the bigger you knows what you really are.

If we are no longer caught up with the ego and we become humble, doesn't that destroy our self-confidence and self-esteem?

No. Humility is not the same as lacking self-respect or feeling worthless, which again arise from seeing ourselves as separate. Humility is not feeling inferior, it is realising our equality. You are as vital to the universe as any other part. Therefore, if you respect the universe, you must respect yourself. Humility is simply a lack of arrogance. Accepting that you are no better or worse than anyone else or anything else can give you the courage and wisdom to live your life well and begin to realise your full potential as a human being.

We have been blessed by being born members of a species with the capacity to see, understand and participate in the whole of creation. Don't attach to it; be it. Observe, play your part with enthusiasm and give all the love you can.

Chapter 11 - Do We Have Free Will?

Again and again, in this book, you will have read about the importance of choice: how stepping back into the Observing Self empowers us to choose what to think, how to act and even what feelings to entertain so that, to a large extent, we can be what we choose to be. As we have seen, this is the true meaning of the word "Freedom", since we are no longer a slave to our thoughts and feelings and can choose our response to the circumstances we find ourselves in.

Yet the idea of choice or free-will has long been a topic of controversy among philosophers. Quite apart from beliefs among the faithful that there is a divine hand shaping the course of our lives and vague inklings among the rest of us about "destiny", "fate" and "luck", resulting in a lucrative trade in horoscopes and suchlike, there are also the assertions of sages and scientists that all time is now and therefore choice is an illusion. When apparently backed up by science and sound reasoning, these arguments, at the very least, call upon us to question the seemingly common sense notion that we are free spirits and able to do whatever we like. But is that logic sound? And what are the implications for ourselves and for society if free will is illusory?

In this chapter, I will give each intriguing hypothesis due consideration. If you choose to explore these deep and turbulent waters with me, at the end you will get to make up your own mind on the subject. Or will you? That's the point. Is your judgment pre-ordained before you even make up your mind? Fascinating isn't it? Let's go exploring.

The Concept of Choice

At every point in time there are choices to be made and the future depends on these choices. One person's choice of career, or partner, or who to vote for, or whether or not to have children, or whether to write that angry letter or sleep on it first, or even where to go on holiday, can have far reaching results for themselves and others.

Can you imagine a world in which Hitler's mum decided not to have children? Or Einstein's dad decided to practice celibacy? Or Martin Luther King decided not to get involved in politics?

Our lives, and those of everyone around us, are continually shaped by our actions, which often result from our decisions. It's something we all take for granted most of the time but it becomes most obvious when things go wrong and we get into the business of "If only..."

Cause and Effect

The most extreme view about our power of choice is the law of cause and effect or: "As ye sow, so shall ye reap," which presupposes that we actually have a choice in what we sow and thereby reap. We have difficulties with this idea when we see villains literally getting away with murder while there are law-abiding people and innocent children suffering wherever we look.

We may try to fix this anomaly by invoking ideas about an afterlife where all scores will, eventually, be settled. This might involve rewards in heaven and punishments in hell, or it might involve reincarnation and karma, endless cycles of birth and rebirth in which our actions have consequences that follow us from life to life. This then provides us with a cop out. We don't have to care about the suffering masses if we convince ourselves that they somehow deserve their misery as punishment for some bad stuff they did in a past life.

And we can also rest easier in our beds knowing that the bad guys will get their comeuppance in the end, whether we, or they, live to see it or not.

Other than by coincidences such as tripping up and twisting an ankle after making an unkind remark, which seem to support such a theory, we really don't have a lot of scientific evidence to back it up.

The Universe and the Multiverse

The same could possibly be said about an offering from the scientific community: the multiverse theory. Though this is now a widely-respected theory, it is pretty much impossible to prove or even to disprove or falsify. In a nutshell, it has been suggested that there are an infinite number of universes in addition to our own, in which there can even be different laws of physics.

One version of this theory is that every time two (or more) possible things can happen, they in fact both happen but, at that instant, the universe splits into two and while we trot along happily in the version where we avoided getting run over by that bus, there's another one out there, parallel with ours and somehow occupying the same space but maybe in a different dimension, in which we were not so fortunate. That universe has since divided into one where we spent some time in casualty and were then sent home, and one in which we no longer feature, and so on. It's a bit like a soap where the writers can't make up their minds between their different ideas for the series so they make the whole lot and run them in different rooms, all at the same time.

As the theory goes, there are an infinite number of universes and anything that could have happened has happened somewhere, and anything that can happen is happening now.

It would not be terribly surprising if you found this idea a bit unsettling. What bothers me most about it is that, if it is true then, even as I strive to keep my loved ones safe from harm, in some other dimension I may not have succeeded. Of course, the reverse is true. If you have lost someone dear to you, perhaps you might gain some comfort from knowing that, in countless alternative universes, they are still alive and well and sharing their life with you.

Uncomfortable or not, at least multiverse theory doesn't exactly rule out the possibility of free will, since we only perceive the time strand we are currently in, so from our point of view, we do have choices and we are living in the universe we choose. Of course there may be occasions when someone else makes our choices for us, or when accidents thwart our intentions, but that still doesn't invalidate the concept of free will.

What may be even more unsettling is the idea that the future has already happened.

Spacetime as a Loaf of Bread

Looking at a single universe, some scientists are telling us that the whole of spacetime exists all at once and that past and present are illusions that we each create as we move through it, which seems to imply that all our future decisions are already made, together with all their resulting outcomes, but we just can't see them from where we are standing in the here and now.

This, to most rational people, must surely sound like nonsense. Practitioners of mindfulness will tell you that the present moment is all we have. The past is over and no longer exists (and our memories of it are less accurate than we imagine) and the future hasn't happened yet, so of course it doesn't exist. We live in the now, and when we keep our attention right here, without worrying about the past or the future, our lives become immeasurably richer.

So if that's obvious, what do we make of the argument proposed by cosmologists that spacetime is a four-dimensional chunk, like a loaf of bread in which each slice is a particular instant in time? The loaf is all there but we only see our particular slice of it as we progress through the loaf.

Relativity and Free Will

Strange as this may sound, when you look at the implications of Einstein's theories of relativity, with time passing at different rates for different occupants of the cosmos, depending on their relative positions in spacetime and the speeds at which they are travelling, things do start to get seriously weird, and the notion that our particular 'now' is as applicable to Andromedans as it is to us Milky Wayans (and the guy in the wormhole connecting them, and the crew of an intergalactic starship a few billion light years away from either of them) doesn't necessarily hold up. As we saw in the chapter on science, this would certainly make the lives of Captains James T. Kirk and Jean-Luc Picard infinitely more complicated than we fondly imagine, with or without warp drive, but most of us can happily avoid thinking about such issues in order to avoid over-taxing our brains, unless our space-travel technology ever progresses to a point that makes it relevant to us personally.

In theory, as we saw when we discussed relativity, if we could travel at a more substantial fraction of the speed of light, we could go for a little spin in our starship and come back to find that everyone we knew and loved had long since grown old and died while we were still in our prime. To the then occupants of Earth, if any still remained, we would have travelled forwards in time, even though for us and for them, life would have seemed to progress at a normal pace. So who's idea of 'now' would be valid. And if each is equally valid, what about the universal now?

For a fascinating account of this, do read *The Fabric of the Cosmos* by Brian Greene. Here's a quote: "The only thing that's real is the whole of spacetime."

As Einstein once said: "For we convinced physicists, the distinction between past, present and future is only an illusion, however persistent."

If this is true then the multiverse theory actually becomes more reassuring. Taking it to its logical conclusion, it would mean that all possible future outcomes of all decisions yet to come are already in existence, and therefore inevitable, but at least it provides us with some measure of control of our own destiny by allowing us to choose which forks to take in the road and thereby actively select the particular timeline we wish to live in.

Deterministic Laws and the Measurement Problem

Physicists have another slightly worrying idea, however: the deterministic nature of the laws of physics. According to this theory, once we know all the laws of physics, we can predict exactly what will happen, anywhere, any time. An apple doesn't choose to fall off a tree, it just grows according to its nature until it gets too heavy for the twig, or the wind applies a bit of extra force, or someone comes along and picks it. If we knew all the variables involved, we could predict the exact moment of its detachment from the tree.

The classical laws of physics seem to point to determinism. Even quantum theory, famous for its Uncertainty Principle and the fuzzy realm of probabilities, suggests a similar possibility. However, despite the amazing accuracy of the Schrödinger equation when it comes to predicting what the subatomic world will get up to at any given instant, not all physicists agree that this means that the entire universe, including our own behaviour, is deterministic, and one reason for this is the fact that the presence of an observer appears to influence the behaviour of the sub-atomic world.

This suggests that perhaps we do have some say in what goes on after all and it is not necessarily justifiable to say that we can ever predict the future with any degree of accuracy or that the whole thing is already fixed in the fabric of space-time.

What the Neuroscientists Say

For anyone still championing the concept of free will, a major setback cropped up during the eighties when a neuroscientist, Benjamin Libet, conducted a series of experiments in which participants sat in front of a timer. They had EEG electrodes attached to their heads so that their brain signals could be monitored as they performed the simple task of pressing a button and typing in the time on the clock face at the moment they became consciously aware of the decision to move.

The results showed that there was a very small, but seemingly significant, delay between the start of increased activity on the EEG printout and the moment the participant became aware of making a conscious choice to press the button. For many years, this has been widely interpreted as evidence that the idea of conscious choice is an illusion. This interpretation was still being extolled at a conference I attended in 2016, though in my opinion, and that of many others in recent years, the experiment seemed deeply flawed. The half a second delay could be explained in various ways, not least of which is the time it would take to place attention on the task, intend to make a decision, think about the decision, make that decision and then register the time, send another signal to the motor neurons that move the finger and press the button. This lengthy process would be expected to show up as the "readiness potential" that was indeed

211

observed and does not suggest that the decision was made from some mysterious source over which we have neither control nor awareness.

It is incredibly difficult for us to specify the exact moment in which we make up our mind about something. To be able to then record this to the nearest millisecond may assume a degree of reliability and skill that is beyond our capabilities. It also assumes that decisions arise very quickly and surely and that we don't spend a moment or two dithering and doubting first. We have to question exactly what is going on during that "readiness potential" phase of recorded brain activity.

In subsequent experiments by others, participants have been provided with two buttons and asked to press one or the other in response to images on a computer screen. In these experiments, the readiness potential was seen to occur before the images actually appeared on the screen, which suggests that the brain activity did not relate to the actual decision being made but perhaps to a general intention to move as soon the image finally appeared. In other experiments, the readiness potential was also observed in participants who decided not to move at all. It has been suggested that the readiness potential arises in an area of the brain that we use when we imagine moving, rather than the area responsible for actually using our conscious will to perform an action.

So, personally, I am not at all convinced that these experiments cast doubt on the existence of free will. If anything, they appear to support it. The readiness potential seems to be an area worthy of further investigation, however, since it may provide useful insights into the changes taking place in the brain when we direct our attention and make use of our faculties of imagination and intention.

What the Ancient Sages Say

Strangely, some interpretations of Eastern philosophies actually support the idea that everything is pre-ordained and free will is an illusion. How is this possible when they also speak of Karma (and the responsibility that implies), and mindfulness or living in the moment rather than an illusory past or future?

The argument goes something like this:

If there is only one Self and everything is a part of that Self, then that same Self is in everyone and is the impartial witness which looks out through the eyes of the patient and the nurse, the murderer and the victim, the thief and the judge, without being affected by any of it. It does not make judgements or decisions, it just watches while the drama plays out according to natural laws and the inherent nature, conditioning and karma of the illusory participants, knowing that the whole show, including the characters through which it observes that show, are illusory.

This suggests, to some scholars, that we have no choice in what we do in any given situation: we simply act according to our genetic tendencies, upbringing and life experiences and even when we go against the grain, for example when a habitual thief decides not to burgle that house after all, it's still an inevitable consequence of some influence they have been exposed to which put the idea of honesty into their head.

Ethics

Let's think of the implications of this. If it were true that we really have no choice in anything we do, would that mean that we also have no responsibility for our actions?

213

What effect would that have on our Criminal Justice systems? If no one could ever be deemed to be responsible for their actions, then how could we hold criminals accountable and punish them for their crimes?

And if, as some philosophers say, nothing matters anyway because the whole thing is an illusion, no more real than a dream, does that give us the right to go out and do whatever we like, irrespective of any harm caused to other illusory beings by our own illusory being?

This idea was explored by Fantasy writer Stephen Donaldson who, in *The Chronicles of Thomas Covenant, the Unbeliever*, created a breath-taking saga about a man who goes to sleep and wakes up in a different world, which he takes to be some kind of lucid dream. Should he do whatever he likes, regardless of the consequences for the other inhabitants of the dream world? Or does he still have some kind of moral responsibility to help them in their need, whether or not he believes them to be real?

We are all presented with this ethical dilemma if we interpret the above theory in a certain way: imagining the Self as a passive, uncaring, unfeeling, impotent witness to the passing show. From this interpretation, it follows that when bad stuff happens and we cry out: "God, how can you let this happen?", the stony silence we receive is because God really doesn't care one way or the other and couldn't intervene anyway, being only a passive witness to our illusory lives and our concerns in our illusory world.

Having no responsibility would no doubt rid us of a fair amount of guilt. Can you imagine a world in which every bad thing you ever did was OK because none of it was real anyway? Could we completely dispense with the idea of a conscience? On the other hand, it would probably rid us of a fair amount of motivation too. What would happen to the concepts of success and achievement if we were all hapless slaves to our conditioning and had no choice about the good things we did any more than the bad ones? Would our lives not become completely pointless?

What a gloomy idea! But while the deterministic argument seems to carry a lot of clout, being espoused by a fair number of scientists and occasional popular gurus, it doesn't quite ring true does it?

Another View

If we get to the heart of what it is that makes us uncomfortable with the above ideas, we may find that it is not a black and white issue (ie free will or not free will): our confusion may boil down to a question of interpretation.

If we truly are all one, which has been suggested so many times by so many people (or perhaps through one voice that speaks through all of them), then one is one and not two. For there to be an illusion witnessed by a passive observer, there must be two: the observer and the illusion. If there is only One, then the illusion is the observer and the observer is looking at itself.

In this case, for those who are interested in the God analogy, God can't dismiss us as an illusion because God is also us. Our concerns are therefore God's concerns because we are all God. This is the same as saying that our concerns are the Self's concerns because they are all the Self. How could we be anything other than our self? If not, who would we be?

The confusion only arises when we have unhelpful ideas about who and what we are. As we have seen in previous chapters, these ideas are generated by what is often known as the ego. Our individual little self - with its body and its collection of hurts and pleasures, opinions, beliefs and concerns - thinks that that is all there is to it, forgetting the greater Self which gave rise to it and of which it is still a part. This is

215

much like a wave forgetting it is ocean or a finger forgetting it is part of a body.

It is this idea which is the illusion, and the sages from all parts of the world have urged us to see through this and remember what we really are. As we have seen, this is the so-called "Perennial Philosophy" which is at the root of most religions, though in most cases long forgotten.

It is the ego which is subject to the laws of determinism, being driven by instinctive urges, addictions, desires, aversions, conditioned responses and habits and a whole bagful of beliefs which it has acquired on its journey so far.

The Self in us can see through this. When we step back far enough, seeing the body, senses, emotions and mind as instruments available for our use, things change quite radically. We can notice the content of our minds and observe the tricks they get up to, but we are no longer under the delusion that this is all that we are. When we are free from this delusion, we become like a driver taking back control of the car instead of sitting in the passenger seat and allowing it to career down the hill on whatever path the laws of physics decree that it must follow.

Without the interference of the ego - the drive shaft with an over-inflated sense of self-importance thinking that it is calling all the shots - the instrument can be seen to be under the control of the driver and it can work perfectly. It is then that we can make real choices, do what needs to be done in the moment and take responsibility for our actions, within the framework of our deeper awareness that we all are, always have been and always will be, One.

It follows from this that criminal activity is a result of ignorance. We should, however, be careful to define what we mean by a 'crime', since many laws are also the result of ignorance. Not all prisoners are guilty of anything that a rational person would define as morally wrong. For example, should a person found in possession of a small amount of cannabis, or someone carrying out a particular activity without being born a member of the permitted gender, receive the same harsh sentence as a serial killer? Much depends on who decides what is lawful, whether the restrictions we place on a given population are necessary and whether the punishments subsequently meted out to those who transgress are merited.

When I speak of a crime here, therefore, I am referring to any deliberate action which causes harm to other people, animals or property, rather than to actions that are contrary to the prejudices of a ruling elite. Using this definition, we can only commit crimes when we see ourselves as separate. Being all-one, alone, who is there to harm but our Self?

Can the Self Make Choices?

We could ask: since thoughts occur in the higher cortex of the brain, and the Self is beyond these thoughts and is able to observe the content of the mind, how can the Self choose anything?

The Self observes, therefore the Self decides where to rest it's attention. And what it gives attention to grows and becomes reality for that instrument, or the aspect of itself through which it is observing. This is a creative process and our individual thoughts, when they arrive from the stillness of the Self deep within us, are inspired thoughts.

Inspiration is the language of the Self. Ask any great musician, writer, gardener or artist: "who is it that created your works of art?" and they will tell you: "It wasn't me. I just stood back and let something higher work through me". That's how it feels when our real Self is in the driving seat. As we have seen, when we work in this way, we call it

217

"flow". Great athletes talk about such experiences. So do healers, sages, inspired leaders and teachers. This is what it is to be fully human and to truly have the freedom of choice.

Chapter 12 - A Question of Beliefs

Having free will is not simply about having the freedom to make choices about what we do as we go about our daily lives, it is also about having the freedom to change any beliefs that are limiting us or doing us harm: to undo any unhelpful conditioning and to be the kind of person we choose to be. The power to do this comes, not from other people, not from therapists, teachers or gurus, but from the deepest source of our own being.

While we still identify ourselves as a little suffering body with all its conditioned habits and preferences running constantly in the background like old software programmes that we forgot to shut down, clogging up our hard drive and draining energy from our batteries, we may feel helpless and stuck.

When we see our real identity as the source of our individual ray, we can step back towards the centre and look at our own programming more objectively. Without getting bogged down in any kind of counter-productive psychoanalysis and introspection, we can simply begin to notice which beliefs are useful and which are unhelpful, to ourselves and to our species, and we can perhaps see that there is one particular viewpoint that makes sense of it all: the view from the centre, from which we can see that our fellow rays are simply other aspects of our true Self.

I'm not here to ask you to change your beliefs. This book is about exploration, not indoctrination. The following is simply an opportunity to reflect on why we believe what we do and which beliefs might be helpful or unhelpful to us.

Given our previous discussion about the nature of truth and the difficulties that we have in knowing anything with one hundred percent certainty, how do we know which, if any, of our beliefs are true?

How many of our beliefs did we inherit from our parents, our culture or our society? We can answer this fairly quickly by asking ourselves, as we did at the end of chapter four, if we would be likely to hold the same beliefs if we had been born to different parents in a different country.

How many beliefs do we hold just in case they might be true and we don't dare to disbelieve them – such as the possibility of life after death?

Have we ever doubted the prevailing beliefs among the people around us yet been too afraid to speak about our doubts in case we might be ostracised by our social group, or even killed, for voicing them?

Are there any beliefs that we hold onto in the face of overwhelming scientific evidence to the contrary? Or disbelieve when there is overwhelming scientific consensus that they are true?

Are there even some beliefs that we hold onto in the face of our own direct experience to the contrary?

Might there be some beliefs that we lay claim to in order to justify our own wants and desires? For example, do we ever hide our own prejudices and aversions by referring to similar levels of intolerance attributed to an almighty deity in some holy book? Do we even attempt to do this sometimes when such notions are not actually to be found anywhere inside our holy book?

Do we, perhaps, tend to surround ourselves in a kind of cocoon of people that we trust to agree with us, in person or online, rather than risk having to consider alternative viewpoints?

Our view of reality is distorted by maps and filters and most of us have no idea how they even got there, yet the beliefs we hold affect the way we live our lives and interact with other people.

The stories we tell ourselves about our world can empower us or limit us. It is even possible that we don't recognise the ways in which our beliefs limit us. For example, an elderly lady insisted: "I can't lift my knees far enough to stamp my feet like this," while lifting her knees and stamping her feet to show us the thing that she couldn't do. Another insisted that she could not lift her hand higher than her shoulder, then was seen that same day reaching up with that same arm to take something from a high shelf in the supermarket. A gentleman said that he could not possibly put a heel down before his toes while performing a gentle exercise sequence, due to an anatomical difficulty, and then proceeded to walk out of the room at the end of the session heel to toe. If we don't believe we can do something, there's a chance that we won't even try and our belief that we can't do it can actually blind us to the abilities we already have.

Success comes from repeatedly trying and learning from our errors until we either get to where we planned to be or to somewhere unplanned, yet equally helpful, that emerged during the process. At the very least, we may learn what not to do next time. What inspires us to have a go is a vision of what is possible – and these boundaries can strreeeetch!

However, there are many reasons for not allowing our limiting beliefs to stretch, as psychologists have discovered. For example, we appear to have an inbuilt survival mechanism that programmes us to fit in with the people around us as far as possible, even if the people around us are strangers.

The widely-evidenced 'bystander effect' has shown us that the more people there are present at the scene of a street crime or medical emergency, the less likely anyone is to intervene or call for help. We seem to look to each other for cues and, if nobody else is doing anything, we may feel less inclined to take any kind of personal responsibility. We may assume that someone else must have called the police or an ambulance, or would have done what needed doing if anything could have been done. If not, we can still feel a bit easier in our minds if we tell ourselves that we were not the only ones who looked the other way. We may even have a fear of doing the wrong thing, potentially making matters worse, or worry about looking stupid when there are other people around to judge us.

This habit may have helped us to survive as a species by seeking safety in numbers and avoiding drawing potentially hostile attention to ourselves. On a wider scale, in our global society with its constant surveillance and data-collection by our ruling elites, our best method of self-protection may be our anonymity. However, our instinct to keep our heads down and go along with the crowd may not be in our best interests at this present time, particularly if it prevents us from raising our concerns about the global situation, for no better reason than that nobody else appears to be doing anything.

On a more hopeful note, however, the bystander effect has recently been called into question by Richard Philpot of Lancaster University. As reported in *New Scientist* in July, 2019, he and his colleagues have studied CCTV footage of violent incidents in the UK, South Africa and the Netherlands. In ninety percent of cases, they found that at least one person tried to help. Moreover, they found that, the more people were present, the more likely it was that someone would intervene – which is the opposite of what we would expect if the bystander effect were true!

Whether the theory was wrong, or whether people are simply changing with the times, remains to be seen. It could be that we are getting braver or more socially responsible. Perhaps we feel more interconnected due to modern communications technology and social media. When witnessing a crime, perhaps we may feel less likely to turn away than to record the incident on our mobile phones, or to intervene so that our inaction does not become a subject of debate when someone else's video goes viral on YouTube. Maybe we simply care more about each other these days or are more altruistic than we have given ourselves credit for, or perhaps our present generation is less socially inhibited than that of our forebears. Maybe we all respond differently, depending on the situation, and this, together with a host of other variables, makes it difficult to lump us all together and conclude that human beings always act in expected ways. Or maybe we have all heard so much about the bystander effect, over the past sixty years, that we have developed an unconscious determination to prove it wrong!

I would like to think that the new research is evidence of our underlying humanity. Perhaps it shows that our global society is evolving in ways that make it more likely that we have the courage and initiative to help each other when the chips are down. We may feel braver when there are lots of us working together than when we feel isolated and powerless – hence, the political policy of 'divide and rule! We may have evolved to a point where we are more ready to take the lead in difficult situations and we may be even more ready to follow such a leader when we see someone step up and try to do something. Sometimes, it only needs one person speaking out to act as a catalyst that gives a kind of psychological permission for others to follow them.

Even then, it is not always clear which leader to follow. We may go along with the opinions of what we perceive to be the majority, even if that perceived 'majority' is actually a small number of people who happened to be allocated more media coverage than the actual majority enjoyed. In an attempt to keep news items unbiased, one person quoting a badly-researched scientific paper may be given the same amount of air space as one person drawing upon thousands of well-researched studies that disagree, giving audiences the impression that the arguments are of equal merit and we are free to make up our minds about which side to take, depending on our gut feelings about the interviewee. We may even vote against someone who espouses a belief we actually share, just because we have an even stronger belief that we should never trust the promises of politicians who claim to support our position, especially if the credibility of that person has been undermined by a deliberate smear campaign, engineered by the owners of whatever news sources we tend to follow.

Our motives are often complex and not always obvious, even to ourselves. When it comes to ingrained beliefs that we have held for many years, we may hold on to them with a tenacity that is resistant to any suggestion of an alternative viewpoint.

Recent research has shown that people actually experience physical and emotional pain when they consider alternatives to their most cherished beliefs. In a study by Kaplan, Gimbel and Harris, the beliefs of participants were challenged while activity in their brains was observed using a functional MRI scanner. The areas that lit up when ordinary facts were challenged were those associated with memory-checking. However, when religious or political beliefs were challenged, the areas that lit up were those associated with emotions and identity.

It is as if our political and religious beliefs are somehow part of our sense of who we are, and we are more inclined to believe something because it 'feels right' to us than because we have studied the subject in depth and made a reasoned decision, based on all the evidence. Questioning those beliefs makes us feel extremely uncomfortable so, even if we are wrong, we will still fight our corner, as an individual or as a nation. We will protect those beliefs at all costs by ignoring, denying or rationalizing any new information that doesn't fit in with them. Instead of modifying our ideas about reality in line with any new evidence, we tend to cling to our old beliefs, however irrational they now seem to others, and try to make reality fit with them.

If all these beliefs that we defend so strenuously were very clear-cut, logical and consistent, we might find it relatively simple to explore and explain them, but the situation is more complicated than that. Would it surprise you to learn that most of us, without even realising it, may have double standards?

A mismatch between what we feel we should do and what we enjoy doing can be problematic for us as individuals and as a species. We may choose to adopt a healthy lifestyle, yet continue to smoke, to drink alcohol and to eat food containing lots of refined sugars. We may feel very concerned about air pollution and global warming yet continue to drive a car and fly to remote destinations for our holidays every year. A sense of guilt, or even distress, may arise when we recognise this disconnect between our beliefs, feelings and actions. Psychologists call this 'cognitive dissonance'.

Some subjects might be, potentially, so upsetting that we would rather close any conversations about them with "I don't want to know", then turn away and just get on with the day-to-day practicalities of our lives. Some of us may be entirely unaware of our double standards. If we do recognise them, we may try to minimise our discomfort by distancing ourselves from their perceived source so that we remain calm and able to function. We may see the adverse effects of climate change, for example, as something that is a problem for other people, in distant parts of the world, or in the far future, rather than accept that this is happening now and it affects all of us. George Marshall, in a book called *Don't Even Think About It*, has studied in great depth how our brains seem to be wired to ignore climate change despite all the available evidence. We may know in our hearts what we need to do to play our part in averting this crisis yet be unwilling to consider it because our personal needs, desires, customs and habits are too strong.

For example, few people, unless they were starving, would kill and eat their family pet, yet, in most countries, a majority of people, unless they have chosen to follow a vegetarian or vegan diet, feel that it is perfectly acceptable to eat various farmed animals just because they like the taste of their meat. They may justify this double standard by saying, for example, that pigs are less intelligent than dogs and that they don't feel pain as much as dogs or humans and, in any case, they are kept in nice conditions and killed humanely, aren't they? And surely we must eat meat in order to get enough protein? Wrong on all counts, yet we may cling to these irrational ideas if we strongly believe that we cannot live without pork or bacon.

In some countries, for religious reasons, it may be unacceptable to eat meat from a pig or a cow, yet be perfectly acceptable to eat the meat from sheep, goats, horses, chickens and even dogs, without considering the suffering of the animals or any consequences for the environment or the sustainability of food resources. Our moral standpoint on such matters will be very much dependent upon the beliefs and customs of the people we were raised among, how much we personally enjoy eating various types of meat and how much thought we have given to living on plant-based alternatives. In extreme situations, such as when starving in a desert, our need to stay alive may override our principles and the most committed vegan might kill and eat a rabbit, or their pet, or even resort to cannibalism. Though some may prefer to die rather than compromise their values in that way, in general, we may justify different behaviours and different levels of concern for animal welfare, depending on the circumstances.

We do the same with people. For example, we are bombarded by daily news of human suffering in all parts of the world and the scale of it is just too much to cope with as we try to go about our daily lives, so we tend to push most of it out of our minds unless it is very close to home and we realise that the people we see suffering on the news could have been our own community, or our own family, which makes it more real to us than when it happens on the other side of the world. To see every person on the planet as part of our own global family would require us to make a leap in our perception that few of us would be prepared to make. The heartbreak and sense of responsibility would be overwhelming.

And of course, it is this tendency to distance ourselves from things that make us feel guilty or uncomfortable that makes it possible for some of us to carry out diabolical deeds and justify them by telling ourselves that some people are less than human; or allows some of us to get on with playing games, following celebrities and living the good life by holding on to a belief that distant suffering, or even the destruction of the global environment, does not concern us.

What would it take for us to stand up together, as a global species, and say: "We will not permit this"?

Actually, it is already happening. Amazingly, it is our children who are taking the lead in showing us what is possible. Only today, the 15th March 2019, as I write this, hundreds of thousands of school children and students across the globe have taken to the streets of our cities to demand that governments take action on climate change. While many of us have developed the habit of shaking our heads in despair and wondering what is to be done about the problems we face, one sixteen year old girl, Greta Thunberg, decided to sit outside the

Swedish Parliament every Friday. Within weeks, the youth of the world had been inspired to follow her example. Though not yet old enough to vote, they are calling on our governments to wake up and do something.

According to the newspapers this week, the youth activists behind the protests have told decision-makers that:

> *"We are going to change the fate of humanity, whether you like it or not. Our generation grew up with climate change and we will have to deal with it for the rest of our lives. Despite that fact, most of us are not included in the local and global decision-making process. We will no longer accept this injustice. The youth of this world has started to move and we will not rest again."*

For too long, we have been limited by our belief that one person can do nothing in the face of such huge challenges. Now, however, we are seeing what is possible and it is no longer appropriate for us to sit watching TV and hope that other people will sort it all out.

We can stand with the people of every war-torn nation. We can stand with the victims of violence, abuse and misogyny. We can stand with the orangutans in their burning forests and refuse to buy products containing palm oil. We can stand with all the animals enduring brief and hellish lives so that we can have meat, eggs and dairy produce. We can stand with the people who are begging us to leave fossil fuels in the ground and invest in alternative sources of energy. We can stand with the planet Earth as its surface is ravaged and depleted of topsoil, edible vegetation and drinking water and we can say: "Enough!"

We are not limited individuals. We are one human race and we can speak with one voice if we choose to.

What do We Mean by 'Morality'

So how do we know what is right or wrong?

Our core beliefs include our values: our morals or ethics. If we choose to make a stand for what is right, how do we know that we are 'doing the right thing'?

Are your values something you were born with? Were they learned from your parents, your teachers, your peers or religious leaders, or from the media, books or films?

Or are they something you came to feel for yourself after experiencing distress while witnessing the suffering of others? Do you, perhaps, have your own moral code which is something along the lines of: "Do unto others as you would have them do unto you," or "Morality is living in a way that does not cause any harm to others and perhaps even improves their quality of life"?

When some kind of thought or idea arises in the mind - maybe as a result of something we heard from a parent, a teacher, a friend, the media or some other source - we may become attached to it and take ownership of it so that it becomes our own opinion, even without any evidence to support it. As we have seen, we may then screen out any evidence to the contrary and seek support for our opinion from other people until it becomes a belief. Any new thoughts, experiences and ideas may then be influenced by the beliefs we already hold until we become so entrenched in our particular world-view that we are prepared to do more or less anything to defend it, including going to war and killing other people who hold a different set of beliefs.

If beliefs were simply ideas in our own minds and stayed there without causing any harm to anyone, perhaps it wouldn't matter what we believed. Unfortunately, however, our beliefs direct our actions and our actions do affect other people, but how do we know which beliefs are helpful or harmful? If going along with the majority is not always the best idea, do we check the facts and the science? Do we, as a minimum, make sure that any actions arising from them will not cause harm to others? Is our underlying sense of values strong enough to guide us through times of crisis and uncertainty?

We can decide to be 'politically correct' or respect the beliefs of others because we are told to do so, while at the same time harbouring an undercurrent of doubt and resentment that bubbles to the surface in times of perceived crisis. Or we can have a genuine respect for all life and all human beings, arising from our awareness that we all emanate from one source, and so treat everyone as our own Self: a view in line with the old 'do as you would be done by' motto but arising as a consequence of our perceived oneness.

Of course, that doesn't mean that we have to tolerate behaviour that puts the safety and lives of others at risk but we need to be very clear about whether our perceptions of risk are accurate or whether they arise from unconscious biases against certain people or groups of people.

It may be that much of our prejudice against people who do not share our beliefs comes from our fear of the possible actions that we think they might take as a result of their beliefs: actions which we imagine may threaten our lives, our loved ones, our livelihood, our lifestyle or our standards of human decency. Whether or not this perceived danger actually exists, perhaps the fear of such consequences may be so powerful that it overrules reason and causes us to act in the very ways we feared that they would act.

When our own beliefs are the kind which compel us to behave in ways that are harmful to ourselves, to other people, to other creatures, or to the planet we live on, then perhaps we might want to think about taking a fresh look at them and asking if there might be other viewpoints which could be more helpful to us, as individuals and as a species.

Even then, we need to be careful. If we decide what to believe in advance, we may invent rationalisations and seek justifications that take us round in circles and back to the mind-set we started with. This can lead to all sorts of problems such as religious bigotry and a blind refusal to examine anything unfamiliar or unknown. Anything that goes against our pre-existing expectations may then be rejected and anything that appears to support them may be accepted without scrutiny.

Instead of asking ourselves, "Does this feel right?" we need to ask ourselves, "Is this true?" and "How do we know?"

If we are to find the truth, we need to be humble enough to put aside any vanity, insincerity or hypocrisy and let go of our attachment to whatever it was that we were expecting to learn. That is the only way that we can come to see things as they actually are rather than as we wish them to be.

When we think that we have discovered a truth, we must examine it from every angle. If something is true, then it will stand up to every kind of scrutiny. If it doesn't, and we discover that we were wrong, we should welcome that. A dead end often forces us to look in other directions and opens up new, and possibly more fruitful, lines of enquiry.

"Truth has nothing to fear from fullness of investigation."

Dr. Paul Brunton

Helpful or Unhelpful?

The following are a few examples of some beliefs for you to consider.

This is not a question of which are "right or wrong" or what we "ought to" believe. We can simply ask ourselves which of the following are the most helpful to us if we choose to ensure the continued survival of our own species and of life on this planet.

1. We are completely separate from the world and from each other.

2. We are all made of the same 'stuff' and are interdependent.

1. It doesn't matter how we treat each other.

2. When we hurt each other, we hurt ourselves, since we are not separate, we are all one.

1. The universe is made of matter, which is mostly lifeless and inanimate and floats around in an empty vacuum.

2. The universe is a continuum, possibly composed of dark energy and dark matter, which we can't see, and light matter which we can see. On a subatomic level, all of it is made from vibrating energy, including own bodies, which constantly renew themselves by exchanging energy (as food, heat, air etc.) with their surroundings. The atoms that make up our bodies were created in the hearts of suns. We are not just in the universe, we are part of it. We are one with the universe.

1. Only the human brain has sufficient complexity to allow it to be aware of its own existence. Mind is an 'epiphenomenon' arising from matter inside the brain.

2. Since the universe includes all human brains as well as everything else, then it must, by definition, also be complex enough to be aware

of its own existence. Perhaps matter is an 'epiphenomenon' arising from mind.

1. Everything happens by random chance and there is nothing we can do about it.

2. Quantum Physics has shown us that events at a sub-atomic level are influenced by the presence and intentions of an observer. There may be much that we can do to direct the flow of change and alter our experience of reality.

1. Mankind was given dominion over the Earth and therefore has a right to exploit and use its resources for his own purposes.

2. As the one species with the freedom of movement, skills and intelligence to affect the global environment at will, mankind has the responsibility to guard and respect all life and to preserve the beauty of the earth for its own sake as well as for future generations. What we do to the Earth affects us. We are one with the Earth and with all living and non-living things.

1. Some people are superior to others and can use and exploit them as commodities on the basis of gender, race, class or any other reason they consider to be valid.

2. All human beings have equal value and none have the right to harm or exploit others. We can rejoice in our diversity while at the same time knowing that we are all one, and behaving accordingly.

1. There is a God who is separate from man and can be loving but can also be vengeful and jealous and who needs and requires us to do particular things to keep Him happy and to earn His rewards after we die, and this may involve killing other people.

2. If there is a universal field of fields which is conscious of its own existence and from which everything arose, then we are all part of it and are one with it. If we call this "God" then God is everything and,

being everything, God needs nothing. Nothing is required of us. However, if we choose to be happy and to survive as a species, we must require of ourselves that we live in peace with each other.

1. We will either be rewarded in heaven or punished in hell after we die, depending on how we behave in this lifetime.

2. We create heaven-on-Earth and hell-on-Earth by the way we treat each other and our planet. This is not a divine reward or punishment, it's the natural consequence of the choices we make.

1. The best way to change people's behaviour is to punish them, take away their freedom or threaten them with violence or eternal damnation.

2. Since the actions of people arise from their beliefs, the only way to encourage people to respect each other and live together in peace is to enable them to widen their viewpoint to include the possibility that we are all one.

1. People are born sinners and atonement is the way to seek forgiveness for those sins.

2. The word 'sin' was originally an archery term meaning 'missing the mark'. The evil acts we do are only possible because we see ourselves as separate and our own needs as more important than anyone else's. When we re-member that we are all connected, there is at-one-ment.

Now imagine a world in which a majority of children grow up with many of the beliefs listed as 1. above. Then imagine a world in which a majority of children grow up with the beliefs listed as 2.

Which would you choose?

Part 4 – Creating The Future

The Prophecy of Chief Crazy Horse

*"Upon suffering beyond suffering; the Red Nation shall rise
again and it shall be a blessing for a sick world. A world
filled with broken promises, selfishness and separations. A
world longing for light again. I see a time of seven
generations when all the colors of mankind will gather under
the sacred Tree of Life and the whole Earth will become one
circle again. In that day there will be those among the Lakota
who will carry knowledge and understanding of unity among
all living things, and the young white ones will come to those
of my people and ask for this wisdom. I salute the light within
your eyes where the whole universe dwells. For when you are
at that center within you and I am that place within me, we
shall be as one."*

*This is a statement of Crazy Horse as he sat smoking the
sacred pipe at Paha Sapa with Sitting Bull for the last time,
four days before he was assassinated (Sept 1, 1877)*

Looking back at my own life and the permanent changes that took
place back in 1993 when I experienced the paradigm shift that
transformed my view of pretty much everything, I would say that the
most immediately obvious effects were the disappearance of my fear
of death and an awareness that the empty ache of unfulfilment, despair
and misery deep inside me simply wasn't there anymore. Basically, I
was happy. Along with these two things came an urge to help others
to find relief from their suffering and find that same inner contentment
and wholeness. I didn't want anyone else to be alone and afraid in the

last moments of their life, whether that be on a hospital trolley in a corridor, as I was, or at a roadside or wherever else they happened to be when they realised that it was about to be 'game over'. I didn't want anyone else to go through their life feeling empty or scared or helpless when my own experience told me that it didn't have to be that way.

What might we expect to happen, individually and as a species, if all of us, or at least a sufficient number of us, were to become 'enlightened'? What might the world be like? What difference would it make to our lives and our present situation? Would we be happier? Would we communicate differently? Would we, perhaps, discover new ways to influence our reality and shape our future? What do you think?

Let's explore these intriguing possibilities together.

Chapter 13 - Being Happy

What is Happiness?

I have met people who tell me that they have never been happy in their whole lives. How is that even possible? Have they really never been happy, or do we all perhaps have different ideas about what happiness might be? Might we be dissatisfied with mere contentment because we are looking for something else that we can't quite define? What do we even mean by the word 'happiness'? What do you think happiness is?

Would it surprise you if I said that happiness is a decision?

OK so I need to explain that if I'm to keep my promise of not just coming out with pithy, BS-like statements.

What I mean is that, the way I have come to see it, the reason we find happiness so difficult to find is that we are looking for it 'out there'. We do that because we tend to confuse it with pleasure and there is a commonly-held belief that things and people can 'make us happy'.

To consider this more closely, we can begin by looking at what kinds of things give people pleasure.

The possibilities here are endless, but some examples might be:

Being in love.

Listening to music.

Driving a new car.

Winning the lottery.

Having lots of beautiful possessions, comfort, luxury.

All of these things can give us a temporary rush of chemicals, such as dopamine, that create feelings of elation and well-being. Of course, there is nothing wrong with these feelings, in themselves. Our problems begin when we become overly attached to anything that gives us these feelings and believe that we can't be happy without them.

Particular difficulties arise if our desire for pleasure is accompanied by a need to possess something or someone or we become addicted to things which we know to be harmful to our health, or to other people.

If two people look at a beautiful garden, one might think: "I wish I had a garden like that", feel jealous of the owner, and feel discontented as a result. The other person might think: "How lovely", be happy for the person who owns the garden and be grateful for the experience of seeing it and thankful for all the work the owner put into creating it for others to see. The second person might then go about their own life without envy or resentment or any desire to possess a garden like that, though it may inspire them to create something beautiful themselves one day. Ironically, freeing ourselves from the desire to possess things allows us to feel that we own the whole world.

Unfortunately, sources of pleasure can easily become the most important things in our lives. In fact, they can effectively take over our lives so that we spend all our spare time thinking about where our next bit of pleasure is going to come from. For example:

The next thing we are going to buy.

The next holiday we are going on.

The next promotion in our job.

The next bar of chocolate / cup of coffee / cigarette.

The next chance we will have to get our "ideal partner" to take an interest in us.

We may expect that if we get these things they will make us happy. Certainly, they often give us a feeling of pleasure - but how long does the pleasure last?

The holiday comes to an end. The latest cars and clothes become last year's models and designs. The 'ideal partner' turns out to be a real person with a mind and faults of their own, which makes it impossible for them to live up to our unrealistic expectations. And even if we win the lottery, there is always that awareness that there are some things that money can't buy.

Usually it doesn't even take that long for the dissatisfaction to set in. It's as if the anticipation and the brief rush of chemicals at the moment we acquire a thing we wanted are more important to us than the thing itself.

When the pleasure wears off, it is natural to immediately look for another source of pleasure: buy something else quickly, even in some cases before we are out of the shop where we bought the first thing! Online retailers make use of this by bombarding us with suggestions of what else we might like to buy at every stage of our visit to their site: before, during and after we reach their checkout and thereafter through a deluge of junk mail and irritating pop-up menus on our screens. In the same way, we might feel the need to find a new partner, buy a new car, move on up the career or housing ladder. We mustn't fall behind or we could become poor, unpopular, lonely, bored. And then we would be unhappy. Wouldn't we?

It's a bit like being at the fun fair. We can imagine any source of pleasure as a Ferris wheel that we jump onto when it's on its way up, forgetting that we must, inevitably, go over the top and come back down the other side. If we don't like the sensation of coming down,

239

because coming down makes us feel cheated and disappointed, we might jump onto a nearby wheel that is on its way up. If there are lots of Ferris wheels standing next to each other, all rotating in the same direction, we can keep jumping onto another and another so that we never really come down very far but keep riding the crest of the wheels like a roller coaster. This is a pretty fair approximation of the lives of many people in our society today, with or without the encouragement of the media and advertisers, who are very happy for us to continue to play this game.

Some of us may spend more time down at the bottom of the wheels than others, but even when we're not up there riding high we can spend a lot of time and energy wishing we were. (This is desire).

So if riding the roller coaster is not the same as being happy, how do we get off? Does it mean that we should give up trying to be happy and spend all our time being poor, bored, lonely and depressed? The answer lies in looking again at the Ferris wheels. What we have here is a series of circles. The top of each is something positive and attractive, the bottom is it's opposite, something negative that we really don't want.

Perhaps this might remind you of the Chinese Tai Chi symbol, the yin and the yang 'fishes' in the circle. Isn't this exactly what we're talking about?

We can't stay in the yang region forever, life won't let us do that. And trying to stay in the yin region isn't a viable alternative. But there is another solution. Notice the still point at the centre of the circle, which everything revolves around. This is Wu Chi, the point of balance, peace, stillness, harmony, serenity and equanimity. When we stand here, we can watch the whole thing revolving around us and not be caught up in it. If we join the dots at the centre of each circle, from Ferris wheel to Ferris wheel, we find a straight line: a steadiness that can allow us to navigate our way through life on an even keel and so avoid many of the highs and lows that can sometimes make our lives so difficult.

We can look at life without too much attachment; just watch and see how life is, with all its ups and downs. We can learn to understand it. We can let go of excessive desires, addictions and self-pity. We can appreciate beautiful things and feel happy for others who take pleasure in possessing them, without needing to possess them ourselves. We don't need to resent people who have more wealth or status than we have, or gloat over any good fortune that comes our way. We can accept people as they are and not try to possess them or expect them to be perfect or superhuman. We can see that everything changes and stop trying to cling to things and keep them exactly as they are. We can enjoy small things, natural things, which don't cost any money, like sunsets and flowers and making other people happy. We can look at what we already have and feel lucky and content with that.

This doesn't mean that we can never fall in love, or buy a new car, or attempt to change things for the better, or that we won't get old or sick. We can still live our lives to the full but without excessive attachment or aversion. A gold necklace or a dirty floor cloth are neither good things nor bad things in themselves, it's how we see them that gives us problems. Everything is ultimately made of the same stuff, the same sub-atomic transient packets of energy, so why love one thing and hate another? We can decide that we like the shape of a cup better than a plate but they both have their uses and they are both made of the same clay.

Why bother to look at the world in this way? Because the roller coaster ride doesn't make people happy. Standing in the centre does. When you see that pleasure and pain are both temporary and opposite sides of the same coin, you are no longer bound by them and you create the space to be yourself and make your own decisions instead of feeling that you are caught up in forces you can't control. This leads to a deep and lasting sense of contentment and happiness from which you can get on and enjoy your life and help others to do the same.

How to Be Happy

We can allow ourselves to be happy if we let it happen now. Sources of pleasure, as well as being fleeting and impermanent, are also very often seen as being things for the future. We say "I will be happy one day when I get that job, buy that house, marry that person, divorce this person, have children, lose some weight, get my hair done, win that game, pay off the mortgage, win the lottery..."

Happiness is not dependent on luck or wish-fulfilment. Happiness is a decision that we make in this moment. Right here. Right now. If we can make that decision to be content with what we have, right here, right now, we don't have to wait to be happy.

All of the above can be worked out just by following a logical argument and looking for examples in our own lives to test whether or not it is true. Just by replacing our need for the dopamine rush with an attitude of gratitude, we can go a long way towards improving our inner well-being. Enlightenment, however, takes us naturally to this state, without even requiring us to fathom it all out. If our unhappiness came from a perceived lack of something, then the cause is taken away when we realise our oneness with everything. How can we lack anything if we already are everything? How can we go seeking for something when what we are looking for is what we already are?

If what you are looking for includes more peace, love and joy, then you can be happy to know that all of these are available to you right now. When the clouds of doubt blow away, you can rest deeply in the peace, love and joy of your own being.

Chapter 14 - Love as Real Communication

"Dislike of a person excludes the possibility of understanding them and blinds the faculty of insight."

Dr. Paul Brunton

When we discover the peace, love and joy that lies at the heart of every one of us, it tends to 'rub off' on the people around us. You may know of people you would naturally go to if you were sad or had a problem: the unflappable ones, the wise ones, the ones who make you feel more calm and reassure you that everything is going to be OK and help you to look for workable solutions; the ones who care about you and take the time to listen.

The greatest gift we can give to another person is our undivided, loving attention. By really being there for someone, in the present moment, without wanting to be somewhere else or trying to influence them in order to make them fit in with our own ideas of what they should be or do, we 'real-ize' them; we help them to feel real, special, valued and cared for. In such moments, two beings re-cognise each other (or know each other again): Self meets Self and something amazing happens. It can be like coming home; a union, a healing. I and thou become an 'I-Thou', just as two notes of music can merge in harmonic resonance. The Self is simply present in two forms and is experienced as love.

Couples can live together for decades yet never share this kind of connection. Even service may be seen as duty, expected of us by society or by the person we are serving, or performed for some kind of reward such as financial security or perhaps a guaranteed place in heaven. When it arises directly from love, from genuine communication with another human being, it is pure service and arises

244

spontaneously out of a desire to help the other person to be safe and happy, with nothing expected in return, as a mother may be with her child. The best carers are like this and I have had the privilege of knowing many of them in this lifetime.

When we begin to communicate with people in this way, we may also begin to glimpse our oneness with everyone, and when we begin to see the oneness of everything we may begin to communicate with others from a basis of unconditional love, whether we are talking about our nearest and dearest or a passing stranger on the street.

In our society, many human beings have a tendency to form groups. Some groups exist for convenience or safety or economic gain. They come in all kinds: the staff of an organisation, for example, or a club, a society, a community, a class, a team or whatever. Some groups are useful, others pathological, and it's not always easy to know which sort you are getting into before you join them.

The difference may stem from whether the group is a collective, in which everyone sharing a particular characteristic is lumped together and expected to conform to the requirements of the group, or a community, in which the individual strengths, ideas and characteristics of each person are valued and the group achieves its mutual aims through cooperation, though much will depend on what those shared aims are.

Love within a group is a logical consequence of the meeting of two or more people who all share the ability to communicate by offering their presence, without the expectation of anything in return. Just being there for each other in that moment, without pre-judgement or expectations, creates a space in which each person can give and receive attention and feel valued and cared for.

Being accepted by a group empowers us to be ourselves and to accept others in return, therefore love grows and, while individual qualities and personalities are appreciated and treasured, stereotypes and biases begin to fall away and an awareness of the oneness within everyone can become increasingly apparent.

Love is like a light that always shines but seems to dim when ideas of separation obscure it. By spending time in this light, each group member becomes stronger and more at peace and gains the spare capacity to go out and create that space for others by offering their loving presence and undivided attention.

I think that there is an inherent need within most people to belong to a group or community where this process can happen safely; a group where no one has a vested interest in the 'conversion', manipulation or exploitation of its members and where the overall aim of the group is benevolent, altruistic and meaningful.

Inevitably, of course, there will be some groups that deliberately exploit this need. People may be drawn into cults or gangs which seem to offer a supportive and understanding environment yet cultivate a dependence that leaves them unable to think for themselves and alienated against rival groups or outsiders generally.

This is something to be very much aware of if you consider yourself to be on some kind of spiritual quest, such as we are engaged in now. There are so many 'gurus' and organisations out there who are happy to take your money, claim to have all the answers you seek, and then ensnare you in a subtle web of obligation, restrictions and even separation from your loved ones. As people become more wary of such cults, newer outfits may not even say that they have 'spiritual' motives but may advertise what they do as 'self-help therapy courses' or 'professional development workshops'. Common ingredients of the latter include sleep deprivation: "Those of you who are really dedicated will stay behind to watch this optional three-hour video and be up with the larks next morning to meditate or go for a run with your fellow participants before the next day's work begins." You are likely to come away buzzing and ready to convert everyone you see to this new ideology and follow the helpful suggestions made by the organisers, which will normally include the investment of a large sum of money to prove your commitment, which promises a large return in the future but is more than likely to be some kind of Ponzi scheme which benefits only the person controlling the show.

In a group that is working well, people are free to come and go as they please, there is no dependence, only empowerment, and there is nothing to be gained from 'converting' other people. The still point in a hurricane has nothing to gain from being still; it is simply still and thus provides refuge from the storm. A well in the desert has nothing to gain by being full of water, it is just its nature and, simply by being itself, it provides without judgement. In the same way, a person who has been fortunate enough to recognise his or her connectedness to the source is like an oasis in the desert or a ray of sunlight among the clouds.

Perhaps, by reading this book, or as a result of your life experiences so far, you may have become aware that you, yourself, are the source of this sunlight.

Compassion and Cooperation

Let's now try to imagine living in a global society in which a majority of people recognise their connection with each other and with the planet and act accordingly. What might that be like?

Are we entering the realms of pure science fiction or fantasy here? Are the habits of greed, selfishness, violence, aggression, jealousy and all the rest of our 'dark side' so ingrained into our nature that we are doomed to continue to cause suffering wherever we go? Would we be doing the universal community a favour if we wiped ourselves out at this point?

Well, when you watch the news each day, you could be forgiven for thinking so but, strangely, research into such matters leads us to a different conclusion. Researchers have found that a majority of people are altruistic, often putting the needs of other people before their own.

In studies of various tragic disasters all over the world, from the attack on the twin towers in New York to hotel fires, sinking ships and earthquakes, there was no evidence of the primitive 'every man for himself' mentality that we may have come to expect from the way human nature is so often portrayed in the media and the movies. What researchers found is that many of those who were able to remain calm enough to save themselves also tried to help others. Often the greatest reason for loss of life was that a majority of people froze and were unable to move, even when others were trying to encourage them to get into lifeboats or leave a burning building.

In terms of what we know about the brain from previous chapters, this is what is usually called the 'fight or flight' response but is actually better named the 'fight, flight, freeze' response. As discussed by Michael Bond in *New Scientist* in May 2017, research has shown that, in an emergency, most people are trying to think with the emotional area of their brain, the limbic system, which sees things in very simple, black and white terms and finds it difficult to absorb and deal with new information and decisions. Escaping from an aircraft or building is easier if you have already rehearsed the evacuation procedure and know what to do, otherwise the emotional brain gets stuck trying to figure it all out in a real emergency.

People naturally try to cooperate with each other under various circumstances in which they are faced with a difficult challenge. In the famous Robbers' Cave experiment, often referred to as a 'real-life

Lord of the Flies', in which groups of teenage boys were left on an island, the results were flawed due to the bias of researchers, who tried to deliberately engineer conflict between the groups to prove that we are an aggressive and territorial species. In fact the boys naturally started cooperating and sharing, despite deliberately engineered provocation, and eventually turned against the researchers, who were subsequently discredited.

It would be easy to imagine a bunch of alien scientists watching us to see how we will handle our present situation, like some huge reality TV show with us as the stars. We can perhaps see them rushing to get home each evening to see how many creative ways we have found to bring about our own demise. How satisfying might it be to do something they don't expect and show ourselves to be a benevolent and compassionate species who are more than capable of working together to find practical solutions to our difficulties?

We can do this, folks! We are not inherently bad people. Although we still appear to be climbing the evolutionary ladder, our collective intelligence has come a long way over the last century or so and we are both cleverer and kinder that we tend to give ourselves credit for.

"Then it was as if I suddenly saw the secret beauty of their hearts, the depths where neither sin nor desire can reach, the person that each one is in God's eyes. If only they could see themselves as they really are. If only we could see each other that way there would be no reason for war, for hatred, for cruelty...we would fall down and worship each other."

Thomas Merton

Chapter 15 - The Creative Process

Whether we create our world consciously or unconsciously, that process of creation goes on, for better or worse.

As the great mathematician and physicist, John Wheeler, said:

> *"The universe does not exist "out there," independent of us. We are inescapably involved in bringing about that which appears to be happening. We are not only observers. We are participators. In some strange sense, this is a participatory universe."*

Since we know that reality is not what we think it is, maybe we need to consider the possibility that, perhaps, what we think is what reality is.

If our thoughts are, in any way, involved in creating our reality, is it possible that we can consciously choose to change our reality, or at least change our perception of reality, which kind of amounts to the same thing?

If so, how could that be possible? What evidence do we have to support that idea?

For anyone who has explored a thing called 'abundance theory' – the idea that there is enough of everything available in this world for all of us to manifest everything we ever dreamed of if we believe it strongly enough – and came away with misgivings when we saw that we are actually using up resources at double the rate that our planet can sustain, it may not seem credible that we have much of a say in changing our reality for the better.

We might look at the tiny percentage of our global population controlling the vast proportion of its wealth and wonder how this unequal distribution is in any way fair. We might read best-selling books that tell us the secrets of financial success, and their sequels that tell us that if we are not yet rich, it's because we didn't want it hard enough. While some of us may consider it indecent for a few to have so much wealth while others struggle and starve, a few may justify their good fortune by quoting the law of attraction, in much the same way as the law of karma, or cause and effect, can be used by some to dismiss the misfortunes of others as something they deserved as a result of their bad behaviour in past lifetimes or their lack of initiative in this one. Both of these ideas can, potentially, be misused as cop-outs for human decency and responsibility.

However, that doesn't mean that we are entirely powerless to change our lives and our world for the better. The following are some of the ways in which what we do with our minds might influence not only our view of reality but also our actual experience of it.

They are easy to remember because they all begin with vowels:

A Attention

E Expectation

I Intention

O Obviousness

U Unity

We'll start with one that is so self-evident that most of us already know it at an instinctive level, whether we have consciously thought of it or not. As discussed at the *New Scientist* conference in 2018, scientists engaged in research into consciousness are now very much aware that one of the main influences that shape our perception of reality is the power of expectation.

The Power of Expectation

You may have heard the famous story about an old woman sitting beside the road at the edge of a town. A person comes along and asks her what the people in this town are like.

"What were the people like in your home town?" she asks.

"Oh they were awful!" says the traveller. "Liars, cheats, rogues. You couldn't trust any of them. To be honest with you, I was glad to see the back of them."

The old woman shakes her head and says: "You'll find the people in this town just the same."

A few minutes later, another traveller passes by and asks the old woman the same question.

"What were the people like in your hometown?" she asks.

"Wonderful!" exclaims the traveller. "Honest, hardworking, loving, kind. I was sad to leave them."

The old woman nods her head and says: "You'll find the people in this town just the same."

You don't need me to tell you that people tend to live up to our expectations of them.

If we don't give people a chance to show their worth or we constantly criticise them, making them nervous with our own hostility and jumping on every slip they make as evidence of their incompetence, we can't be too surprised when they get cross with us and act in ways we disapprove of even more. It's bad enough if we do this to our work colleagues and neighbours but worse when we do it to our spouses and especially to our children, since they have more invested in our approval and the effects of our negative expectations are therefore more far-reaching.

On the other hand, you will probably have noticed how, when we look for the best in people, make allowances for their errors and give them an opportunity to shine, we can watch their confidence and self-esteem grow and see them flourish as the fine people they are.

You have probably heard of a famous experiment by Rosenthal and Jacobson in the sixties, involving a group of schoolchildren who spent time with teachers who had been told that some of them, who were actually selected at random, were very bright and gifted 'spurters' while the others were 'undesignated' and so could not be expected to do well. Although the teachers were instructed not to tell the children about these differences, the children soon began to live up to the teachers' expectations. At the end of the academic year, 1964-65, the 'spurters' were judged by their teachers as having "a better chance of being successful in later life", and as being "happier, more curious and more interesting than other children". They were also seen to be "more appealing, better adjusted and more affectionate", "less in need of social approval" and "more alive and autonomous intellectually".

This experiment had been conducted in order to find out if a child's education could be affected by social disadvantage due to lower expectations of their teachers. One can only imagine the damage done to the self-esteem of the 'undesignated' children, including those who, in spite of the experiment, managed to gain high results in IQ tests yet, according to Rosenthal and Jacobson, the higher they scored, "the less favourably they were rated by their teachers". In other words, achieving against the teachers' expectations was seen to be "undesirable behaviour". This came to be known as the Pygmalion Effect and has alarming implications for our modern society.

A similar study was conducted by a teacher called Jane Elliott in 1968. The children in her class were split up on the basis of their eye colour and each group spent a day being told that they were superior to the others. The children performed significantly better in simple tests on the day when their eye colour was judged to be superior. They also became arrogant, bossy and unpleasant towards their classmates, while those with a different eye colour became more timid, isolated and subservient. This study was controversial because it gave us very disturbing insights into the potential effects of discrimination, conscious or unconscious, including racism. Two documentaries were made about Elliott's experiment: *The Eye of the Storm* and *A Class Divided*, which was filmed fifteen years later.

These examples illustrate how our expectations become self-fulfilling prophecies.

What's not always so apparent is the way we also do this to ourselves. If we are constantly beating ourselves up for the things we think we do badly and telling ourselves that we are no-hopers who will never amount to much, we limit ourselves and live up to our own poor expectations.

If we expect other people to dislike us or to avoid us then, by our behaviour towards them, we make that dislike and avoidance more likely; whereas if we expect them to be friendly, we will probably feel more at ease in their company, smile more and so increase the probability that they will warm to us and behave in the friendly manner we anticipated.

For some people, the fear of rejection grows into a kind of social phobia, where they are terrified of making a speech or going to parties in case they make fools of themselves and, because they are so scared, they create the bad impression they dreaded. I think most of us have probably been there! Fortunately, like any skill, our social skills tend to increase with practice, especially when we begin to consider the feelings of other people first instead of obsessing about what they might think of us! No one is easier to make friends with than someone who genuinely cares about our well-being.

Even the physical circumstances we find ourselves in may be influenced, sometimes, by this self-fulfilling prophecy effect: from the photocopier that has a habit of breaking down every time you go near it to the job you didn't expect to get and so didn't.

If you are into reading daily horoscopes, you may be very aware of this phenomenon. I once knew a gentleman who wouldn't go out of the house on days when his horoscope was particularly worrying. Perhaps they should be called horrorscopes!

This doesn't mean that we should go around with daft grins on our faces and be disgustingly (and unrealistically) positive all the time, and I in no way wish to suggest that we all get what we deserve. None of us can sit back in luxury and say that the millions of suffering people in our world today brought it all upon themselves by the sins they committed in their past lives or by their negative expectations.

What I am suggesting is that we may all have a far greater ability than we realise to create opportunities to improve our circumstances, self-esteem and relationships with other people simply by being more aware of the effect of our expectations on all aspects of our lives.

This knowledge can be very empowering, as can all of the insights we will discuss here; which brings us to the next one on our list: the power of Attention

The Power of Attention

To illustrate how powerful this one is, we can do a brief experiment. Rest between each step.

1. If you are able to lift one hand to shoulder height, with your arm relaxed and gently outstretched in front of you, do that now and then lower your hand down slowly, allowing your fingers to trail behind as you lift and lower your wrist. Do it again a few times to "get the feel of it".

2. Then do it again a few more times, and this time inhale as your hand comes up and exhale as it comes back down. Just close your eyes and focus on your breathing as the hand rises and falls. Then do the same thing in reverse, exhaling as the hand comes up and inhaling as it comes down. Is there a difference?

3. Now do the same action again but this time focus all your attention in the palm of your hand as it rises and falls.

4. For the next one, place your attention on the skin on the back of your hand, noticing perhaps whether your hand feels lighter or heavier as it moves up or down.

5. Lastly, with your eyes still closed, just notice how the air feels as your hand moves through it.

What did you discover?

Had there been someone watching you, they probably wouldn't have noticed much difference each time you lifted and lowered your arm. It would have looked like the same action repeated many times. But did it feel the same to you every time? Or did the experience change, depending on where you focussed your attention?

If you answered "yes" to that last question, I would not be surprised, as I have done similar exercises with thousands of people over three decades, and virtually all of them have said "yes".

Some people say they found that their hand or arm felt lighter or heavier or warmer or cooler at certain times during the exercise. Some enjoy one variation more than another. But the empowering discovery we can make from this is that our experience changes, depending on where we rest our attention!

This is not just true of lifting an arm, it's true of life in general. What we put our attention on grows and becomes our reality.

During this exercise, if you chose to do it, your attention was directed by you in response to the list of suggestions above, but when you think about your normal daily life, who or what directs your attention from moment to moment?

Sometimes your attention may be caught by a sudden loud noise or someone calling your name, or a movement that catches your eye. If you are an employee, you may be told to put your attention on the job you are doing. If you are a student, you may be told to pay attention to what your teacher is saying or to a book you are reading or a computer screen in front of you. If you are a driver, you are obviously expected to put your attention on the road and other road users. At other times there may be nobody ordering you or expecting you to pay attention, yet your attention may move about from one thing to another, perhaps fully absorbed in a movie or a conversation, or totally wrapped up in your own thoughts or daydreams.

What is important here is that, ultimately, you are the one who directs your attention. Others can tell you to pay attention, but nobody can make you follow that instruction, assuming that you are able to do so in the first place. Giving something our undivided attention is a learned skill that tends to improve with practice, though it's development may be impeded by the media, who tend to encourage our children to have the attention span of a gnat.

Only you can decide whether or not to go along with a particular suggestion or instruction. It was you who decided whether or not to lift your arm in the above exercise; you who (through your own sense of responsibility) decides whether or not to pay attention if you are driving a car and you who, if your attention is immersed in dark thoughts and you feel that you are going under for the last time, can choose to focus on more helpful thoughts and change your experience of reality for the better.

Let's summarise that:

Since what you put your attention on grows and becomes your reality, and since you are the one who gets to choose what you rest your attention on, then, at the very least, you have the power to shape your own perception of reality. Your perception of reality influences your expectations which, in turn, become self-fulfilling prophecies, which means that, effectively, you have the power to shape your own reality!

Another ingredient to throw into this creative pot is the power of intention.

The Power of Intention

It's true that sometimes people with the best of intentions may go astray (think of how long New Year's resolutions typically last), and it is also probably true that there are people who have committed the most dreadful crimes who would claim that, from their own particular viewpoint, their intentions were honourable (such as psychopaths, terrorists or extremists believing they were ridding the world of evil while impervious to the evil they themselves were creating by harming fellow human beings). Even so, our intentions may play a considerable role in shaping our lives.

For example, we are far more likely to succeed in this world if we intend to put our best foot forward and have a go instead of giving up at the outset.

If we are ill, we may increase our prospect of recovery if we intend to get better rather than putting all our energy into preparing for the worst. This may be one of the reasons why the placebo effect can be so powerful.

Beyond our *intention* to get better, there is our belief that we will get well, in the light of which we can *expect* to get well and so we focus all of our *attention* on getting well.

This is not a guarantee, of course, but it may certainly skew the odds in our favour, especially when you also consider that our immune system is very much affected by our state of mind. Masses of research has been done on this, including experiments that have shown the influence of stress hormones on killer T cells prior to exams and studies that suggest a link between illness and prolonged periods of feeling helpless and hopeless.

Losing hope has been shown to give rise to the nocebo effect, in which our attention is focused on the opposite of getting better. Health professionals are becoming more aware of this. A doctor might think that the words: "One in fifty people die from this condition," and "Ninety-eight percent of people make a full recovery" are just two ways of saying the same thing, but from a patient's point of view there is a world of difference!

The human mind is an amazing piece of equipment and we have yet to fully appreciate its potential.

Obviousness

Something is obvious to us when we have so much evidence to support our belief that there is no longer any shred of doubt in our minds that it is true. To most people it is obvious that, since the Earth is turning on its axis, the sun will come up tomorrow morning, or that water is wet, or that cows eat grass, or that standing in front of a moving train or jumping off a cliff may not be conducive to our well-being. It's the sort of thing that makes people say, "Well duh!"

That amount of belief is very powerful and vastly outweighs any tentative belief that we might decide to hold just because someone else said so. If it's obvious to us that we will get better, our chances of recovery will probably be greater than if we are trying to hold onto a shred of hope given to us by one person's unsubstantiated words of reassurance.

Faith

"See beyond teachings. Find what speaks truth to your heart.
True faith is within."

L. Ryokan

Faith is often spoken about as a kind of gullibility: an unshakeable belief in matters that are based on unsound or 'unscientific' notions. We could have faith in the existence of purple unicorns but few members of the scientific community might be expected to take us seriously.

However, there are times when faith can be a great thing. It can give us the strength to carry on when all hope seems to have faded away.

"Success is not final. Failure is not fatal.
It is the courage to continue that counts."

Sir Winston Churchill

An unsubstantiated belief in various deities may have given strength to our ancestors during times of crisis and helped to ensure the survival of our species. Today's global crisis far exceeds anything that might have been imagined even by our grandparents. We are going to need all the courage we can muster in order to rise to this challenge, and this courage may arise from faith. This may or may not include faith in various deities, but we will need to have faith in ourselves and faith in each other if we are to work together to create the future we envisage, and perhaps we will require, not simply faith, but a deep and fundamental knowing of the One that lies at the heart of all of us.

Unity

When it comes to our ability to influence our reality and our destiny, the one thing that makes it obvious is Unity.

If we are one with creation, then it is obvious that we must have some level of influence upon how it unfolds, and that very obviousness then increases our ability to influence it, as we have seen above. In general:

What we believe, we perceive.

What we perceive, we receive.

What we receive, we believe.

And on it goes...

This is very much in keeping with what we are learning about our universe through our scientific investigations, especially from the study of matter at a sub-atomic level, which suggests that all possibilities exist until an observer collapses the wave function and makes it 'real'.

Very recent variations of the Schrödinger's Cat thought experiment, as described in *New Scientist* magazine in March 2019, have played about with the number of observers present, inside and outside two or more laboratories, and have come up with mathematical paradoxes that suggest that our ability to collapse wave functions affects events taking place in the space around us, therefore our personal view of reality is relative and relationship-dependent, in much the same way that time is.

We have also seen that our perceived universe may be a hologram and may work like a colossal reality simulator or computer game. Maybe, rather than everything existing at the same time, as per the loaf of bread model, nothing exists but a sea of possibilities and we create our reality as we go along, consciously or unconsciously, by the way we are looking at it.

There are some who would say that the idea of human beings having any control of their destiny is pseudoscience and that it is stretching the bounds of credibility too far to dismiss the idea that we are helpless accidents in a mechanical, predictable starscape, compared with which our existence is virtually irrelevant.

While I in no way give credence to strange notions that threaten to take our understanding of reality back into the dark ages and insulate our children against the body of evidence amassed by scientists over centuries, I do feel that, if there is any possibility that we are capable of influencing our reality in any way, now might be a good time to put this to the test, before global warming, over-population, over-pollution, deforestation, war, disease, poverty, starvation and depleted resources, including soil and fresh water, end the debate for us prematurely.

It is my hope that if one mind focused on a vibrant vision of the future can transform that person's life, as indeed it has for myself and for very many of my students over the years, then such a vision shared by the whole of mankind can, potentially, transform our global situation and increase our chances not only of surviving the next century but also of living together in peace with each other and with our world.

This can only happen if people from every part of the globe share a unifying world view that encompasses and explains all our previous faiths and prejudices, our understandings and misunderstandings, makes sense of them and inspires us towards even greater possibilities than we have previously considered.

Such a world-view may remove some of our dependence upon an external source of help but then it may also allow us to acknowledge our own inner resources and assume a greater sense of responsibility for our own actions, and it may empower us to work together to create the kind of future that our grandchildren can thank us for so that when we pass from this world we can do so without shame or regret, knowing that we have left behind us a world that the next generation will be happy to inherit.

A Vision for the World

What you seek is not simply within yourself, it is your Self. You don't need to go to the ends of the Earth to find it. There is nothing out there to find that is not already here, right now. Nobody can take away that which you already are, always have been and always will be.

You don't need to take my word for it. Looking at the criteria we used when we discussed how we can know what is true, we have a consensus from wise people around the world and across the centuries, from scientists and from the founders of religions, and we can read about it in some of the best-selling books of all time, including the scriptures. All that remains is for all of us to experience it for ourselves.

You are love, you are peace, you are what all of this is, and so is everyone else. See it. Know it. Be it.

In India, they have a word, "Namaste", which means: "The Self in me is that same Self in you: We are One."

As a species, if we all truly looked at the world in this way, we would not need laws and threats and punishments (or promises of rewards in heaven) to control us and prevent us from harming one another or causing irreversible damage to our planet. Standing at the centre and seeing that we are all one, why would anyone feel the need to harm anyone else?

Imagine a world in which we stop comparing ourselves with other people; where we have no need to possess, control or dominate anyone else; where our main focus is to look after each other and look after our planet. Might our actions begin to be guided by love instead of by fear?

Would such a vision give us the inner strength to take responsibility for our own actions instead of relying on some kind of omnipotent 'father figure' to intervene on our behalf or tell us what to do and help us to sort it all out? (Or to blame if it all goes wrong?)

Do we, perhaps, have the capacity to shape our own reality and direct the flow of our own destiny by working together towards a vision of the future that we choose for our species and our planet instead of hurtling blindly towards extinction brought about by our own apathy, greed and fear?

Perhaps it is time for mankind to come of age and for all of us to discover what it is to be fully human. When I look around at the world right now, I can see that this process is already happening and, since you have had the patience to read all of this book, I believe that you have already awoken and have glimpsed for yourself the view from the centre of the sun.

What is the ray of hope for the future of humanity?

You are! We all are. And we are all One.

As it says in the *Bhagavad Gita*:

"I have given thee words of vision and wisdom more secret than hidden mysteries. Ponder them in the silence of thy soul and then, in freedom, do thy will."

Epilogue - Practicalities

This book is about hope. I don't have all the answers when it comes to setting our planet to rights but I do know that our chances of survival are very much tied in to our ability to get on with each other and the willingness of each of us to play our part. While we all see ourselves as separate and don't really care what happens to everyone else or we think that we can just ignore the state of the planet and leave it to other people to sort out then, as Sir David Attenborough pointed out recently: "The collapse of our civilisations and the extinction of much of the natural world is on the horizon." Effectively, we have a choice: either we learn to live and work together for our mutual benefit, or we perish together. And at this moment we still have that choice.

As the world wakes up to the reality of this crisis, it is unsurprising that many people, particularly young people, are beginning to experience increasing stress at the thought of its implications. Psychologists have even started to refer to it as 'eco-anxiety', as if it is some kind of mental health condition rather than a normal response to threat. I do not wish to add to that anxiety. Quite the opposite in fact.

Stress increases when we see a threat and feel powerless to do anything about it. I believe that there is much that we can do, however, if we all agree that we do have a challenge here, then remain calm enough to function during the coming years and work together in positive ways to meet that challenge. The targets being set for us by the world's leading climate experts will be difficult but perhaps not impossible to achieve.

As US Senator, Bernie Sanders, has said: "despair is not an option". Neither is panic. While apathy and cognitive dissonance have been instrumental in getting us into this mess, there is nothing to be gained from recognising the truth of the situation if it locks us into the 'fight, flight or freeze' response of our emotional brains and prevents us from using our rational and creative powers to get ourselves out of it. We can't run away; fighting among ourselves would only make matters worse; and allowing our fear to paralyse us will do nothing to solve any of our current challenges. Perhaps by returning to our own calm centre, we will find the clarity and power to do what needs to be done.

The seven point plan proposed in the December 2018 edition of *New Scientist*, following the latest report from the Intergovernmental Panel on Climate Change, includes: stopping using fossil fuels, in our homes, our cars and our industries; designing eco-friendly buildings; and maybe even undertaking geoengineering projects such as scattering particles in the upper atmosphere to help to cool things down a bit. Those things might seem to be beyond the powers of the average person but that doesn't mean that we can all devolve responsibility to the people with the money and the power. Those of us who are old enough to vote can try to ensure that the people we vote for are committed to saving the planet, rather than billionaires with interests in fossil fuel companies. As we have seen, those who are not yet old enough to vote have recently set us an example in how to bring about global change, with sixteen year old Greta Thunberg making a stand outside her parliament and, within a very short time, being joined by hundreds of thousands of children across the globe. One person, working alone, may feel powerless but one person, inspiring millions, can change the world.

Even with the very best of possible politicians in key roles, our own behaviour will matter in other ways too, from recycling our waste to cutting down on travel, especially air travel, and becoming accustomed to a plant-based diet. We can contribute by insisting that the manufacturers of plastic bottles cut down on their production and recycle them safely after use instead of selling billions of them in third world countries where they are burned, releasing toxic fumes, or dumped in waterways. We can refuse to buy products containing palm oil, thereby preventing further devastation of the rain forests of Indonesia. Our cultural and political systems will need a major overhaul so that everyone has a voice and a chance to contribute ideas and solutions and to play their part in the coming decades. We can start by empowering people, including the women of the world, by providing them with an education and birth control and a fair living wage.

One of the great hopes is that the world's decimated forests can be restored, reclaiming land that has been cleared for raising cattle and allowing things to grow there again. We do have the technology to remove at least some of the carbon from hazardous emissions but there are only a handful of places where this is used so far. We would need thousands more to have much effect on reducing global carbon dioxide levels. Ideally, we need to leave fossil fuels in the ground and prevent their end-products from getting into the atmosphere in the first place, but mopping up the mess we have made will still be a priority. The best way to 'capture' carbon from the air and put it back into the ground is not by building lots of machines to suck it in and drill it into the earth, but by planting more trees, and there will only be enough space to do this if we learn to live without meat and dairy products.

Many people have already realised this, as evidenced by the current increase in vegan restaurants and the widening range of meat-free produce on our supermarket shelves. If we buy these, the market will respond by providing more. It will not be enough to become vegetarian and carry on consuming dairy-based milk, cheese and yogurt: that would still necessitate the breeding of cattle, whether or not we eat their meat as well. If we buy less meat and dairy products, farmers will have to go back to growing crops instead of keeping livestock, just as the fashion industry has all but stopped using animal fur in response to "buyer revulsion".

We can all play some small part in reducing the carbon dioxide, methane and other emissions that are warming the planet and contributing to the droughts that damage forests and the floods that wash away topsoil. Cleaner ways to travel by air and road and sea must be found as a matter of urgency but we, individually, must learn to cut down on the number of journeys we make and use locally grown, seasonal food where possible. A good book I have found recently, with lots of ideas of what we can do, collectively and individually, is *Drawdown: The Most Comprehensive Plan Ever Proposed to Reverse Global Warming*, edited by Paul Hawken but containing suggestions from a huge array of research fellows and writers.

Motivation is a strange thing. Human beings, in fact most living creatures, are designed to seek pleasure and avoid pain. We are also naturally resistant to change because it's so much easier to go on with what we are used to than to try something new. If we have worked all our lives to buy a five bedroomed house, it may be a wrench to downsize to something more environmentally sensible after our kids have left home. If we have become accustomed to holidays abroad several times a year, it may seem inconceivable to take our breaks closer to home. If we are partial to beef burgers, peperoni pizza and bacon sandwiches, we may be convinced that we could never get used to vegan alternatives, especially if we see it as a hardship inflicted upon us by tree-huggers and crazy animal rights activists, but it really isn't that difficult and, when compared with the collapse of civilization, or with extinction, or with the fact that millions are

269

already starving due to the effects of climate change, such sacrifices are perhaps a very small price to pay.

There is no blame involved in our present situation. A century or two ago, when the industrial revolution was just getting started and the world seemed big enough to take everything we throw at it and rich enough to supply everything we choose to take from it, we could be excused for not anticipating that it would end this way. In those days, the individual was a small and largely insignificant voice in the wind. But now we do know that our behaviour has consequences. Now we have an internet which allows the voice of the individual to cause ripples around the world. We have power as consumers, as voters, as policy-makers, as leaders, as human beings with the capacity to affect our world.

Nobody wants to be told what to do. At the moment, in the West at least, most of us are free to make our own choices and of course we value this freedom, and most of us would fight to keep it, but how responsibly we make those choices now will determine the length of time that they are still available to us. Such choices become easier when we hold a wider picture in mind: when, instead of our own self-interest, we see all life as valuable, which is an inevitable consequence of recognising our oneness with everything. This is not communism or collectivism - giving up our autonomy to become an unwitting cog in the machine - it's playing our part well, along with everyone else, for our mutual benefit, and thereby fulfilling our ultimate potential.

A book can provide information and perhaps inspiration. It is my hope that, through reading this book, you may have answered some questions and found yourself asking many more. Like pouring a variety of ingredients into a pot, mixing them together and allowing them to bubble and ferment a little, I hope that all of this information gradually comes together, any sediment falls gently to the bottom and, like a fine wine, you are left with the clarity of vision that allows you to see the world in a way that is helpful to yourself, your loved ones and to mankind as a whole.

Imagine the effect it might have on the world if everyone shared such a vision and worked together, with compassion, mutual respect and tolerance, to turn that vision into our reality.

Let's do it now.

Half The Sky

The work of any girl

Is like a ripple in a pond.

She cannot cure the whole world's ills,

Or wave a magic wand.

The place where she is standing

Is the point where she must start.

Alone in her small corner,

She may strive to play her part.

With courage and compassion

She may live and love and be,

And so set an example

For the few who choose to see,

And if they choose to follow

They may play their parts in turn

And set their own examples

So that everyone can learn.

The wisdom of a girl thus spreads

Unto the farthest shore,

Like ripples flowing outwards

To be felt for evermore.

Recommended Further Reading and Viewing

Ananthaswamy, Anil, The brain's 7D sandcastles could be the key to consciousness. New Scientist, 30th September 2017.

Ball, Philip, *The Strange Link Between the Human Mind and Quantum Physics*. BBC Earth, 16th February 2017 http://www.bbc.com/earth/story/20170215-the-strange-link-between-the-human-mind-and-quantum-physics

Barks, Coleman (translator) with Moyne, John, *The Essential Rumi*. Harper. New edition 2004, ISBN-10: 0062509594, ISBN-13: 978-0062509598

Benson, Herbert, *The Relaxation Response*. Avon Books, 2000. ISBN-10: 0380815958, ISBN-13: 978-0380815951

Bohm, David, *Wholeness and the Implicate Order*. Routledge Classics, 2002. ISBN-10: 0415289793, ISBN-13: 978-0415289795

Bond, Michael, *Ready for Anything: The best strategies to survive a disaster*, New Scientist, 10th May 2017.

Bregman, Rutger, *Utopia for Realists: and how we can get there*. Bloomsbury, 2018. ISBN: 978-1-4088-9321-0

Browne, Grace, Bystander effect: Famous psychology result could be completely wrong. New Scientist, 6th July 2019.

Brunton, Dr. Paul, *The Hidden Teaching Beyond Yoga: A Great Western Philosopher Reveals the Yoga Way to Truth*. Century, 1982. ISBN 0-7126-1550-4

Capra, Fritjof, *The Tao of Physics: An Exploration of the Parallels Between Modern Physics and Eastern Mysticism*. Shambhala; 5th edition (14 Sept. 2010), ISBN-10: 1590308352, ISBN-13: 978-1590308356

Carhart-Harris, Robin L. et al., *Psilocybin for treatment-resistant depression: fMRI-measured brain mechanisms*. Scientific Reports volume 7, Article number: 13187 (2017)

Craven, Greg. *The Most Terrifying Video You'll Ever See*. You Tube. June 2007.

Craven, Greg. *What's the Worst That Could Happen? A Rational Response to the Climate Change Debate*. Perigee, 2009

Covey, Stephen, *The Seven Habits of Highly Effective People*. Simon and Schuster; Reprinted Edition (4 Jan. 2004), ISBN-10: 9780684858395, ISBN-13: 978-0684858395

Cox, Brian and Forshaw, Jeff. *Why Does E=mc2?: (And Why Should We Care?)*. Special Da Capo Press 9 Mar 2010. ISBN-10: 0306819112, ISBN-13: 978-0306819117

Chomsky, Noam C., *How the World Works*. Hamish Hamilton, 2012. ISBN-10: 9780241145388, ISBN-13: 978-0241145388

Curtis, A., *Hypernormalisation*. BBC iPlayer, 2016

Curtis, A., *The Century of the Self*. Documentary series in four parts, broadcast March to April 2002.

H. H. The Dalai Lama, *The Universe in a Single Atom: How science and spirituality can serve our world*. Abacu, 2007. ISBN-10: 1846041058, ISBN-13: 978-1846041051

Dalgleish, Tim, *The Emotional Brain*. Nature. July 2004, Volume 5. Pp582-589

Davies, James, *Cracked: Why Psychiatry is Doing More Harm Than Good*. Icon Books, 2014. ISBN-10: 1848316542, ISBN-13: 978-1848316546

Dyer, Dr. Wayne W., *The Power of Intention: Change the way you look at things and the things you look at will change.* Hay House UK, 2004. ISBN-10: 1401902162, ISBN-13: 978-1401902162

Einstein, Albert. *Einstein on Cosmic Religion and Other Opinions and Aphorisms.* Dover Publications Inc. (27 Jun. 2009) ISBN-10: 0486470105, ISBN-13: 978-0486470108

Einstein, Albert and Calaprice, A., *The New Quotable Einstein.* Princeton University Press, 2005. ISBN-10: 0691120757, ISBN-13: 978-0691120751

Ehrlich, Paul, *The Population Bomb: Population Control or Race To Oblivion.* Ballantine, 1970. ASIN: B001LD5GSG

Extinction Rebellion, *This Is Not A Drill: An Extinction Rebellion Handbook.* Penguin, 13 Jun 2019. ISBN-10: 0141991445, ISBN-13: 978-0141991443

Greene, Brian, *The Fabric of the Cosmos: Space, Time and the Texture of Reality.* Penguin Press Science, 2005. ISBN-10: 9780141011110, ISBN-13: 978-0141011110

Gribbin, John, *In Search of Schrödinger's Cat.* Black Swan; Updated edition 1985, ISBN-10: 9780552125550 , ISBN-13: 978-0552125550

Griffin, J. and Tyrrell, I., *Freedom From Addiction.* Human Givens Publishing, 2005. ISBN: 1-899398-46-5

Harari, Y. N., *21 Lessons for the 21st Century*, Jonathan Cape, 2018. ISBN-10: 9780141024530. ISBN-13: 978-0141024530

Harris, James C., *Social Neuroscience, empathy, brain integration and neurodevelopmental disorders.* Psychology and Behaviour, 79 (2003) 525-531

Hartman Thom, *The Last Hours of Ancient Sunlight: Waking up to personal and global transformation*. Harmony. Revised, updated edition (18 Dec. 2007) ASIN: B000XUDGSK

Hawking, Stephen and Mlodinow, Leonard, *The Grand Design*, Transworld Publishers, 2010. ISBN-10: 9780553819229, ISBN-13: 978-0553819229

Hawking, Stephen, *Brief Answers to the Big Questions: the final book from Stephen Hawking*. Published by John Murray 16 Oct 2018. ISBN-10: 1473695988, ISBN-13: 978-1473695986

Hellenes, Phil, or 'Philhellenes,' *Science Saved My Soul*, YouTube video, 2010. https://www.youtube.com/watch?v=r6w2M50_Xdk

Henderson, Bob. *Is this our first clue to a world beyond quantum theory?* (Online edition: *Reality's Whispers (Have we heard the whisper of reality making itself?)* New Scientist, 11th July 2018

Huxley, Aldous, *The Perennial Philosophy*. Harper Perennial; Reprint edition (28 July 2009), ISBN-10: 0061724947, ISBN-13: 978-0061724947

Kaplan, J.T., Gimbel, S and Harris, S., *Neural correlates of maintaining one's political beliefs in the face of counterevidence*. Scientific Reports 6, Article number 39589, 23rd December 2016.

Klein, N., *The Shock Doctrine: The Rise of Disaster Capitalism*. Penguin, 2007. ISBN-10: 9780141024530, ISBN-13: 978-0141024530

Klein, Naomi, *This Changes Everything: Capitalism vs The Climate*. Penguin. ISBN-10: 0241956188, uISBN-13: 978-0241956182

Kristof, Nicholas D., WuDunn, Sheryl, *Half The Sky: How to Change the World*. Vintage Books Edition, 2010. ISBN-10: 0307387097, ISBN-13: 978-0307387097

Leggett, Trevor, *The Sayings of Daikaku* in *Zen and the Ways*, pp58-62 Original edition published by Charles E Tuttle Company, 1978, Republished by The Buddhist Society (20 April 2017) ISBN-10: 0901032476, ISBN-13: 978-0901032478

Mabry, John R. *The Little Book of the Tao Te Ching*. Thorsons, 1995. ISBN-10: 1852307072, ISBN-13: 978-1852307073

Marshall, George, *Don't Even Think About It: Why Our Brains Are Wired to Ignore Climate Change*. Bloomsbury USA (22 Oct. 2015), ISBN-10: 9781632861023, ISBN-13: 978-1632861023

Millennium Simulation: The Largest Ever Model of the Universe. Particle Physics and Astronomy Research Council. Science Daily, June 4, 2005.

The Millennium Project. Max Planck Institute for Astrophysics https://wwwmpa.mpa-garching.mpg.de/galform/virgo/millennium/

Moawad, H., *Alice in Wonderland Syndrome*, Neurology Times, Aug 10, 2016.

Muscaró, Juan (translator), The Upanishads. Penguin Classics. 1965 ISBN-0-14-044-163-8

Muscaró, Juan (translator), *The Bhagavad Gita*. Penguin Classics. 1962 ISBN-014-044-121-2

Musser, George, *Spooky Action at a Distance*. Scientific American / Farrar, Straus and Giroux; Reprint edition (13 Dec. 2016) ISBN-10: 0374536619, ISBN-13: 978-03745366

Perry, G. *Real-life Lord of the Flies experiment led us up the warpath.* New Scientist 14th February 2018.

Ratey, J., *A User's Guide to the Brain*, Little. Brown and Company, 2001.

Rattray-Taylor, Gordon, *The Biological Time Bomb*. Thames & Hudson 1968. ASIN: B001YTZ

Rattray-Taylor, Gordon, *The Doomsday Book*. Panther, 1972. ISBN-10: 0586036040, ISBN-13: 978-0586036044

Rinpoche, Sogyal, *The Tibetan Book of Living and Dying*. Rider (Classic edition) February 2008. ISBN-10: 1846041058, ISBN-13: 978-1846041051

Rosenthal, R. and Jacobson, L., *Teacher Expectations for the Disadvantaged*. Scientific American, April 1968, Vol. 218, no. 4.

Ross, Stephen et al. *Rapid and sustained symptom reduction following psilocybin treatment for anxiety and depression in patients with life-threatening cancer: a randomized controlled trial.* Journal of Psychopharmacology 2016, Vol. 30(12) 1165–1180

Russell, Bertrand, *Science as an Element in Culture*, The New Statesman 1 (May 24 and 31, 1913) Reprinted as *The Place of Science in a Liberal Education, Mysticism and Logic and Other Essays*, London, Longmans, Green, and Co., pp. 33-25, 1918

Sadhguru, (Vasudev, Jaggi), Brown, Emery N., Zapol, Warren M., Taplin, Edward H., Schiff, Nicholas D., *Memory, Consciousness and Coma: Scientists in Conversation with a Mystic*. Published on YouTube 18 July 2018. Recorded at Sanders Theatre, Harvard Medical School on May 14.

Shariatmadari, D. *A Real-life Lord of the Flies: the troubling legacy of the Robbers Cave experiment*. The Guardian, 16th April, 2018

Schrödinger, Erwin, in *Quantum Questions: Mystical Writings of the World's Great Physicists*. Edited by Ken Wilber. Shambhala Publications; 2nd edition, 2001. ISBN-10: 1570627681, ISBN-13: 978-1570627682

Susskind, Leonard, *The Black Hole War: My Battle with Stephen Hawking to Make the World Safe for Quantum Mechanics*. Back Bay Books; Reprint edition 5 November 2009. ISBN-10: 0316016411, ISBN-13: 978-0316016414

Suzuki, Shunryu, *Zen Mind, Beginner's Mind*. Shambhala. New Edition 2011. ISBN-10: 9781590308493, ISBN-13: 978-1590308493

Tolle, Eckhart, *The Power of Now: A Guide to Spiritual Enlightenment*. Yellow Kite, 2001. ISBN-10: 9780340733509, ISBN-13: 978-0340733509, ASIN: 0340733500

Turin, Luca, et al. *Electron Spin Changes During General Anaesthesia in Drosophila*, Proceedings of the National Academy of Sciences of the United States of America, August 26, 2014 111 (34) E3524-E3533; first published August 11, 2014 https://doi.org/10.1073/pnas.1404387111

Taylor, Steve, *Benjamin Libet and The Denial of Free Will: How Did a Flawed Experiment Become so Influential?* Psychology Today, 5th September 2017

Thunberg, Greta, *No One Is Too Small to Make a Difference*. Penguin, 30 May 2019. ISBN-10: 0141991747, ISBN-13: 978-0141991740

Tyrrell, I. and Griffin, J., *Human Givens: The New Approach to Emotional Health and Clear Thinking*. HG Publishing; 2nd Revised & enlarged edition (Mar. 2013), ISBN-10: 1899398317, ISBN-13: 978-1899398317

Ueshiba, Morihei, *The Art of Peace: Teachings of the Founder of Aikido*. Shambhala Pocket Classics, 1992. ISBN-10: 0877738513, ISBN-13: 978-0877738510

Vedral, Vlatko. *Decoding Reality; The Universe as Quantum Information*. Oxford University Press. 2010. 2nd Edition 2018. ISBN-10: 0198815433, ISBN-13: 978-0198815433

Walsch, Nealle Donald, *Conversations With God: An Uncommon Dialogue Book 1*. Hodder and Stoughton; New edition (6 Feb. 1997), ISBN-10: 0340693258, ISBN-13: 978-0340693254

Waters, Lea., Barsky, A., Ridd, A and Allen, K. *Contemplative Education: A Systematic, Evidence-Based Review of the effect of Meditation Interventions in Schools*. Educational Psychology Review, March 2015, Volume 27, Issue 1, pp 103–134

Watts, Alan, *The Book: The Taboo Against Knowing Who You Are*. Souvenir Press. ISBN: 978-0-28563-853-2

Watts, Alan, *The Nature of Consciousness*. Seminar delivered in 1960. https://www.youtube.com/watch?v=lxFB9YSFyJE

Webb, Richard, *Schrödinger's kittens: new thought experiment breaks quantum theory*. New Scientist, 23rd March, 2019

Wong, S., *Why taking ayahuasca is like having a near-death experience*. New Scientist 22 August 2018

Zohar, Danah, *The Quantum Self*. Flamingo; New edition (25 July 1991), ISBN-10: 0006544266, ISBN-13: 978-0006544265

Zukav, Gary, *The Dancing Wu Li Masters*. Bravo Ltd., 2009. ISBN-10: 0060959681, ISBN-13: 978-0060959685

Zuckerman, Phil, *Atheism, Secularity, and Well-Being: How the Findings of Social Science Counter Negative Stereotypes and Assumptions*. Sociology Compass. 2009 Available via Wiley Online Library https://doi.org/10.1111/j.1751-9020.2009.00247.x.

5 Theories & Predictions on What Lies Outside The Observable Universe. You Tube v. Published by Top5s, 2017. https://m.youtube.com/watch?v=XmhEBiIGPUg

How the Universe is Way Bigger Than You Think. YouTube video. Published by Real Life Lore, 28th April 2017. https://m.youtube.com/watch?v=Iy7NzjCmUf0

The Global Footprint Network (estimates of species extinction and how rapidly we are using the world's resources) https://www.footprintnetwork.org/our-work/ecological-footprint/

The Inner Life of the Cell, (Full Version - Narrated) Produced by XVIVO for Harvard University. Uploaded to YouTube on Jan 9th 2013.

27470010R00165

Printed in Great Britain
by Amazon